We Became Wives
of Happy Husbands

True stories of personal transformation compiled by Darien B. Cooper, with her own comments and questions for contemplation

In collaboration with Anne Kristin Carroll

VICTOR BOOKS

a division of SP Publications, Inc.
WHEATON, ILLINOIS 60187

Second printing, 1976

Bible quotations are from the King James Version unless otherwise noted. Other quotations are from *Amplified Bible* (AMP), © 1965, Zondervan Publishing House; *The New Berkeley Version in Modern English* (BERK), © 1969 by Zondervan Publishing House, Grand Rapids, Mich.; the *New American Standard Bible* (NASB), © 1971, The Lockman Foundation, La Habra, Calif.; *The New International Version: New Testament* (NIV), © 1973, the New York Bible Society International; *The New Testament in Modern English* (PH), © J. B. Phillips 1958, The Macmillan Company. All quotations used by permission.

Library of Congress Catalog Card Number: 76-4314
ISBN: 0-88207-731-7

© 1976 by SP Publications, Inc. World rights reserved
Printed in the United States of America

VICTOR BOOKS
A division of SP Publications, Inc.
P. O. Box 1825 • Wheaton, Ill. 60187

Contents

About Darien Cooper: Married and the mother of three sons, Darien (Dä-'reen) resides in Decatur, Ga., and is known in many Southern cities for her women's Bible classes and lectures. Her seminar series, "Will the Real Woman Please Stand Up?" has pointed thousands of women to richer lives with their husbands. Darien is a graduate of Carson Newman College. Her first book, *You Can Be The Wife* of *Happy Husband* (Victor), was an immediate best seller. This, her second book, is an outgrowth of the first.

About Anne Kristin Carroll: Encouraged Darien Cooper to start this book and collaborated in the preparation of the stories, is married and has two sons. She has assisted Darien in her seminars by sharing her own story, told here in the opening pages.

In loving memory of our
precious friend

XARA WARD

She touched each of our lives
in a different way and brought
each a little closer to Christ.
We look forward to our reunion
with her in heaven.

Introduction

Daylight had hardly broken one morning in early March when the phone rang. As I reached for it, I wondered who would possibly be calling at such an early hour.

When I answered, Anne Carroll's voice greeted me. She said that during the night she had been quite ill and unable to sleep. While lying in bed wondering whether to call her doctor, a thought began to take shape that she decided to share with me.

"Darien," she explained, "I have been thinking more and more about many of the women who attend the seminars or women who began to read your first book but were just not ready to trust God completely for their marriages. I believe that if women could read some of the marital transformations that we hear and see, they would not hesitate to accept God's way and His principles.

"What do you think about putting a variety of true testimonies in a book so that any woman picking it up could in some way identify with at least one of them? When they see that these women, in the same situations or with even more serious problems, were able through Christ's power to turn their lives around, they too would be encouraged to apply God's principles in their lives. I feel deeply that all some women need is hope, and such a book would offer that hope to many."

I agreed with Anne that there was a need in this area, but I expressed my reservations. I was convinced that another person's experiences could not alter a woman's life unless that woman could understand the principles through which these marital innovations took place. Changes might occur as the result of reading someone else's story, through trying to mimic her actions, but these would be short-lived. Lasting changes would not come to pass unless women could understand how to apply God's principles through His power.

We prayed about Anne's idea. In a short time, God impressed my heart as He had Anne's that this book would be in God's will if the principles could be provided at the end of each story. Then women could see that the failures and heartbreaks in these marriages were not a matter of "bad luck" or fate but were a result of violating principles in God's Word. Just as bad luck hadn't caused the marital problems discussed, neither did a sudden turn of fate mend them. Women must see that the turning point in each of the situations came when each woman realized that she alone was totally insufficient to correct the existing problems in her marriage. When she understood how and when to apply the truths set forth in God's Word through His power, then and only then did her life become fulfilling, happy, and complete.

We both felt that it couldn't be stressed enough that changes seldom occur without some pain, and that deep and lasting transformations do not happen overnight. We both know that Christ wants an abundant life for us, but only through consistent reliance on Him and application of His principles can this become a reality.

A few weeks passed as we prayed and talked about the book. Finally we said, "If it is Your will, Lord, that we write this book, You will have to provide us with the women who will be willing to share their testimonies." With little effort on our part, we obtained the stories you are about to read.

We now want to thank all the women who have shared with us the intimate details of their lives. We realize that for many of them it has been extremely painful to go back into the past and relive these heartbreaks and failures. All of the women whose stories are presented here felt as we do, that if their experiences might help even one woman find the peace and happiness they have, then the pain of recounting their lives would be worth it.

For obvious reasons, most names and locales have been

changed to protect identities, but all of the situations, lives, pain, heartbreak, and happiness are real.

We express our appreciation to each of the contributors and also to: Dot Baker and Vivian Price for their excellent and untiring job in editing, and to Anita Spaugh, Annelle Swilling, Lattie Garrett, Jan Kerr, and Peggy Sosebee for typing the manuscript.

Both Anne and I were blessed by the cooperation of our families.

I, Darien, wish to thank my husband and three sons for patiently supporting and loving me, even when I overextend myself and violate the principles I hold so dear.

I, Anne, want to express my deepest love and appreciation to my husband, Jim, for allowing me to write this book. His faith in me and encouragement have meant much during the past months. My sincere thanks to my two sons for all the duties they performed for me so that more of my time could be free.

1

My Journey Back
to Love

Anne Kristin Carroll

While men and women drifted from group to group, mingling, talking, and looking, I sat watching. I was 21, the mother of an infant son, newly divorced, uncertain, searching. The rodeo was in town this chilly midwinter evening, and everyone was sporting his best western attire, from jaunty jeans, shirts and boots to the ultimate in garish, "boudy" Texas style.

I was sitting at a table in Mid Lane Gardens, a bar in the southwest area of Houston. The name doesn't sound illustrious now, but in the early '60s it was one of the "in" spots for singles. Being a nondrinker, I was in very unfamiliar surroundings. Grant, the guy I was currently dating, had brought me here more than once, but I never felt comfortable. I didn't know what was expected of me in this crowd, and whatever was expected I felt I couldn't handle it.

Strains of "Moon River" drifted on the smoky air as people wandered about. Bored and scared, but curious, I left our table and strolled into the other room. There a friendly male voice startled me.

"Hi, there."

"Hi," I replied uncertainly.

My mind whirled as I tried to place where I'd met him. He must have sensed my confusion.

"I'm Jim. We met here last Friday."

Vaguely I remembered him.

"Oh, yes, yes."

The scene flashed back through my mind. I had been sitting at a table with a friend, trying to fit in, and Jim was one of the strangers at the table.

He interrupted my reflections. "Hey, would you like to go to a party?"

He certainly gets to the point, I thought.

"Well," I explained, "my date is in the other room."

Jim dismissed my reasoning. "So what? Mine is, too. Why don't we just split?"

I responded to his positive lead. "Sounds great! Let's go." I really wasn't interested in another Saturday night of fending Grant off.

The party we went to was in one of the singles' complexes in the heart of what some Houstonians called "Sin Alley." The rocking beat of twist music met us as we joined the party. My new date was momentarily appalled to find I didn't know how to dance, but he offered to teach me. Amused at my attempts to learn the twist, he finally suggested: "It's like drying your bottom after a bath without moving your upper part."

But I couldn't seem to coordinate body and feet in anything that resembled dancing. I felt as though I must have been put together differently from the rest of the girls.

I had always felt different. I had no brothers or sisters. My father was 41 when I was born, my mother 31. My parents' friends had no youngsters or else their children were grown, so I spent most of my time with adults. I believed that my Daddy, a successful businessman, could solve any problem and fix anything for me. With him, I felt loved and wanted, and Mother anticipated my every need. Therefore I was never forced to cope with the demanding realities, responsibilities, and consequences of life.

As I remember myself at 13, I looked like a Roman elephant with my protruding ears and patrician nose. Wanting me to feel proud and to help me gain some much-needed confidence, Mother arranged for my protruding ears to be corrected through plastic surgery. I was pleased with my neatly pinned-back ears, but instead of being happy I refocused my inferior feelings on my nose.

At 14, insecurity so plagued me that I once took my mother along to a youth meeting at our new church. Before I was 15, I met Dan, a reserved high school senior. Our dating throughout my last three years in high school gave us both a sense of acceptance without competition.

To many parents I might have seemed like a model child. I didn't smoke or drink, or even go to parties, but spent most of my time in school and church. Mother knew, however, that it wasn't my "goodness" that kept me in line. Perhaps she did not realize that my lack of self-acceptance was my basic problem, but she took me to psychologists, hoping to help me. I made up fanciful stories about their ink-blot pictures, and the doctors asked me interminable questions, all with the same gist: "What do you think are the answers to your fears and insecurities?" I felt like screaming, "I don't want questions! What I need are answers!"

One of the places where I looked for answers was at church. I remember vividly my experience at 12. Our family regularly attended a church where the expressions "making a profession of faith" and "joining the church" were nearly synonymous. Either decision was signified by going to the front of the church sanctuary at the end of the service. Many of my contemporaries had already joined the church, and I decided before a service one evening that tonight was decision night for me.

As the "invitation" began, the front of the church seemed to move farther and farther away, and the aisle grew longer and longer. I kept saying to myself, "I'll go on the next verse of this hymn." Finally I admonished myself, "Self, you're moving out into that aisle."

I did. But it was as if my stomach and heart remained in the pew. Mechanically I walked the aisle and faced the minister at the end of it. He said something like, "Do you believe in Jesus Christ?"

With no real understanding, I answered weakly, "Yes." And I was accepted into the church.

But my problem of feeling worthless and insecure remained. By the time I was a junior in high school, the awareness of a void within drove me to spend more and more time in church. Dan and I still shored each other up, and we often went to meetings together.

At church "revival services" I'd get all charged up—but it wouldn't last. My life was a constant roller coaster: one day I felt beautiful, spiritual, so close to the Lord the way I believed a Christian should feel; the next day the harps stopped playing and the "spirituality" left me.

Troubled because I longed for the life I thought Christianity offered, I sometimes "went forward" in other services. Again I heard the same question, "Do you believe in Jesus Christ?" I always answered, "Yes."

No one ever followed up by asking me whether *I* had any questions. I had been around the religious circuit so long that I knew the pat answers anyway. In fact, I knew all the right Scripture verses and I carried a Bible faithfully. Like the rest of my facade, it was only an act. I didn't know a thing about the role I was playing. Jesus was neither my Saviour nor my Lord.

When I graduated from high school, I faced a new world that was asking me to play a different part. I felt the next thing expected of me was to enroll in college. I chose to attend the University of Houston so I would not have to leave home or Dan. But once there, I could not adjust to the competitive college life and I dropped out.

My sense of worth further damaged, I turned to the prospect that marriage might provide the magic to fulfill my life. Dan and I had dated for three years, and we had seen plenty of movies that showed romance plus marriage equals happiness ever after. Our parents preferred that we wait until Dan had finished college, but after much talking they finally consented, and we were married.

After the newness of marriage wore off, I realized acutely that this was not filling my inner void. We attended a church associated with a Bible college, and the students there radiated peace and happiness—everything that I was searching for. I decided to go to school there and find what they had. When my first attempts failed, I thought, "If I do everything they do and refrain from doing what they don't, I should have what they have." But imitation of their actions didn't give me what they had, and I left school, defeated again.

If that's not the answer, I thought, maybe I need a career. So I went to work for Pan American Airways and stayed on the job until I learned I was pregnant.

Dan's graduation from the university and our baby's birth occurred in the same month. We had never been responsible for anything but our daily schedules, as our parents had always supported us. Now we were faced with parenthood responsibilities and a job for Dan.

It was too much for me. I couldn't cope—perhaps I didn't want to. I had never even held a baby, and the whole idea of motherhood scared me to death. Little Kevin was sick and he cried almost constantly the first few months. The walls of our small apartment seemed to close in on me. Afraid I would do something wrong, I sat up all one night on our living room couch, holding my screaming child. All I could think of was that I would call Mother and go home if we both lasted until morning.

With the first light of day, I phoned. "Mother, I can't handle this. I don't know what to do. The baby is sick. Please come get me."

Dan went with us to Mother's. She and the maid cared for the baby, carefully feeding him with a special formula, holding and soothing him as he struggled with a serious digestive problem. Dan had already elected to go to school for his master's degree. Since the baby's constant crying disturbed his studying, it seemed natural for Dan to move back with his parents.

I wandered about in a daze, with no purpose. Motherhood does not come naturally to all women. I wish someone had explained that to me; I felt like a freak—a failure with my own baby!

By September, boredom and the search for my identity pushed me to take another job with a large international importer. There I compared my appearance with other girls and decided I needed some improvement, so I enrolled at John Robert Powers School of Modeling.

Suddenly I became fascinated with myself. School personnel told me I was very pretty, with real potential for modeling. My long, sandy-blonde hair in a knot made me look like an old-maid school teacher, they said, and changed it to short platinum-blonde. They highlighted my eyes with make-up and taught me how to sit and move gracefully. I emerged from the course a different girl—on the outside.

Following the transformation, I remember the first time I walked into a room full of people. Confident of my good looks, I felt approval from the group. That confirmed my belief that physical attractiveness means acceptance in this competitive world. I clutched this new self-confidence for dear life, feeling nothing else about me had any value. People scared me, I had blown the motherhood role, and I couldn't make it as a wife; but I could control my looks.

My marriage to Dan had deteriorated to weekend visits, and before winter began we were divorced. We used the excuse of "incompatibility." The truth was we didn't have any legitimate grounds for divorce. Looking back, I can't recall any of our conversations while we were married. I cannot think of a time when Dan said "no" to me, and "no" sometimes means, "I care about you."

It amazes me now that no one tried to stop our divorce. No one counseled with us. It was as if we were kids who'd gone steady for a long time and were breaking up. The attachment that we thought was love—that first love which we expected to last forever—bent and broke at the first pro-longed strain. As I think back now, I look at Dan more as a brother that I never had. We are still friends, and I am pleased that he found a marvelous woman with whom he enjoys a happy marriage.

I knew no one else who was divorced, and the awful reality filled me with fright and loneliness. Then another blow hit: doctors diagnosed my dad's illness as cancer. It was unthinkable that my father, who I thought was invincible, could be mortally ill.

My world went into a tail spin and my search for stability and fulfillment became frenzied. That's when I met Jim in the singles' bar, ditched my date, and went off to another party.

Jim was the opposite of Dan in many ways. Dan was quiet and a loner; Jim was carefree, exciting, and gregarious. He was tall, with beautifully broad shoulders and wavy brown hair that dangled a marvelous curl over his forehead. To bring more sophistication into my life, he taught me to drink and to dance. I discovered that he had a self-supporting job, while most of my friends were still supported by their parents. Within six weeks Jim and I were married.

But Jim wasn't any more ready for a real marriage than I. He'd spent years in a military school and his home background was totally different from mine. We had a few good weeks before the newness of a live-in wife wore off and Jim gravitated back to his old group. He began staying out with them, partying until all hours.

Shocked, I tried to force him into the role of a "good husband." Then I discovered I was pregnant. Through that summer and fall I cried and nagged, driving Jim to spend more time away from home.

In late November, uncomfortable with my pregnancy, I drove to my parents' house every morning to see Daddy. One morning as I neared the house I saw an ambulance parked in front. Outside a neighbor sadly informed me: "Your dad just passed away."

I did not cry. I couldn't. My mind accepted only information that I could cope with, and I couldn't accept the new void he would leave. Somehow I lived through the next few days in numb disbelief.

I remember some of the funeral. As a line of mourners came by to pay their last respects, I was screaming in my mind, "This isn't right . . . it can't be . . . get up, Daddy, get up!" But it was real. Daddy was gone.

I believed death wasn't final, but I was sure I couldn't face life without my dad. Who would reassure me now and say, "Sugar, everything will be all right"? I thought, "No one will ever feel I'm special again." Like a long nightmare, I had continual dreams of him. Soon I was sure I had seen Daddy and he was trying to reach me from the next life. So I launched into the dark world of the occult.

As I searched, I became enamored with the writings of Edgar Cayce. I prayed, meditated, and used the various methods to try to contact the spirit world. Because Cayce used Christian terminology, I thought he was giving biblical insights. It never occurred to me that the Bible might give specific directions about horoscopes, spiritist mediums, and the black arts. No one suggested I read such Scriptures as Isaiah 8:19-22 or Isaiah 47:13-15. Cayce and his followers even taught reincarnation of the soul, and my skimpy knowledge of the Bible gave me no clue that Cayce's teachings were diabolical perversions of God's Word. My search for identity continued through this tangle of intellectual Christianity and occult beliefs.

Jim's employer transferred us to Atlanta, Georgia, and we were happy while our two children remained with my mother and we searched for a house. When the children joined us in a rented home, problems flared again. Up to this time, my mother had provided a live-in maid to care for the family, and I had not changed more than ten diapers! Jim, as immature as I, could provide little help for my insecurities, and I spent the next year running back to Mamma. She would bandage my hurts, cheer me up, and off I'd go again until the next crisis. We finally bought a lovely home and things were more pleasant for a while.

But I couldn't leave well enough alone. I would have been ripe for women's lib, had it existed in the early '60s. Home bored me, the children frustrated me, and I wanted a maid again. It seemed logical that a woman as talented as myself should not waste her time in the dull routine of housework! As my interest turned from home, Jim's wandered also. The more independent I became, the more Jim seemed to look for someone who needed him. Obviously, I didn't!

The solution to the new problem seemed simple: I must become smarter, prettier, or sexier than my phantom competition. I say "phantom," because I accused Jim of more things than a romantic superman could have done. At the time I didn't recognize that my main competition was *me*. God says in Proverbs 14:1, "Every wise woman builds her house, but the foolish one tears it down with her own hands." Word by word, and brick by brick, I was tearing it down.

As I became more anxious, I developed into a super-detective. I checked for traces of make-up on his shirt, searched between car seats for hair pins of the wrong color, checked his address book for unfamiliar female names. Or I trailed Jim at a discreet distance to a club, waited a bit, then popped in and feigned surprise at encountering Jim. My sleuthing produced nothing productive.

Instead, my antics often humiliated me. When I chased him down by phone, I might hear Jim's voice in the background yelling, "Hey, I'm not here!" to a buddy who answered my call. Or worse, a bartender gave the guys a chortle with the version: "He says he ain't here."

Jim had good reason to stay away from home. No peace existed there for either of us.

One morning after I'd found traces of lipstick on the shirt he'd worn the evening before, I proceeded with a Spanish-style inquisition.

"Where were you last night?" I asked, knowing full well he hadn't been where he reported.

"Oh, after I finished work I got together with some of my buyers," he replied.

"Really?"

"Why?" he asked.

At a fever pitch, screaming, tears streaming down my face, I dragged out the shirt, pointing a finger at the lipstick stain.

"Look at this! I guess your buyers wear lipstick now!" I said, sarcasm etching each word. "Jim, I can't take any more; I can't stand it; you're driving me crazy!"

After the outburst, I collapsed with a stream of tears.

"I'm sorry," he said as he tried to embrace me and soothe my hurt. I was enraged again that he thought "I'm sorry" could eradicate the waves of pain and humiliation flooding over me. Although he was repentant, episodes like this did nothing to improve our relationship. Jim would leave, feeling guilty; and I would feel crushed.

Distractedly, I thought a new nose might make a difference. I contacted a plastic surgeon back home, left my children with Mother, and by the time Jim found out, I lay in the hospital looking as if a truck had run over my face. I would have done anything for Jim's approval and to bolster my frail self-image.

Being prettier did not entice him to stay home. I lay in bed at night, listening for his car, crying, dying a little as each hour passed. I wondered why I had failed, what I lacked, and I longed for Jim to hold me in his arms and love me.

I remember a scene that ran and reran for many years: I lay in bed yearning and dreading to hear the sound of his car in the driveway. When he did arrive, I found myself torn between painful bitterness because he'd been out and relief because he was home. It's as if two people lived in my body: the one wanting to reach out, forgive and love; the other wracked with icy hate, wanting to turn away. In utter frustration I'd cry, "Why? Why?" And Jim would say, "I don't know."

As this drama unfolded, I was convinced that Jim's "I

don't know" was a cop-out. Not until much later would I realize that he really didn't know. Although he would swear he'd never wander again, this scene was repeated with heart-breaking frequency.

On a visit to my neighborhood doctor, I told him some of my problems and he said, "What you need is a pill."

I said, "Yes, that's what I need."

That began four years of antidepressants, barbiturates, uppers, downers, anything I could legally get my hands on. I lived in a daze. If there were no current problems, I still took the pills because I knew I couldn't cope when a difficulty arose. It seemed logical to me, when I felt nervous, afraid, insecure, that the answer was to relieve the anxiety. Eliminating the source of the problem didn't dawn on me. I was putting medicine on the rash and ignoring the cause. As I became more addicted, there were days when I hardly got out of my bedroom.

During one visit to my mother, I read a newspaper article about the treatment of schizophrenics in a mental institution. I learned I was taking twice the dosage of medication prescribed for them! I said to myself, "Either you belong in the institution or off the pills." I started a do-it-yourself kick— and I did kick the pill habit.

Without the pills, however, problems piled on me again and I fell apart. After searching everywhere for answers to life, I considered one more answer: suicide. One lonely night, with no hope for a life that was any different, I sat down to plan my suicide.

Something deep inside wanted to reach out just once more for help, but where? Only my mother, who had borne the brunt of my childishness and failures, knew our real situation. I had played Miss Super Cool with everyone else, never discussing my deep feelings. Not only had we faked a happy marriage in front of our friends, but I had the feeling that even if I had the humility to call them, they didn't have any answers either.

That seemed to be the longest night of my life. I cried,

then phoned all the social-help numbers in the directory, one by one. I heard, "Pray." Another said, "Christ is the answer." But how? I'd tried all that.

Morning came, and a phone call from a neighbor whom I hardly knew, Xara Ward. The subject of religion came up. Xara said, "I'm going to a ladies' Bible class today. Why don't you go with me?"

I was glad Xara couldn't see my face. I had searched the whole world of religious answers, and the idea of a "ladies' Bible class" was ludicrous to me. But I couldn't reveal my true feelings, and weak with the emotional turmoil of a sleepless night, I agreed to go.

When Xara and I arrived at the class, a young woman was teaching from the book of Ephesians. I thought: What can a housewife named Darien Cooper teach educated, liberated me?

My first impression of Darien was of a tall, slender, obviously intelligent young woman, with a distinct East Tennessee accent which didn't seem to fit the rest of her demeanor. She spoke with authority and yet with such heart-warming knowledge of the Lord. He was obviously her best friend her strength!

As I settled into a chair, I looked around at the women with mixed feelings. Many of them looked happy, and it wasn't fair. What curse had been put on me? With disgust I thought: This Christ-is-the-answer stuff is okay if your problem is the neighbor's dogs upsetting your garbage, or your husband has forgotten your birthday. It wouldn't work if you had problems like mine!

I don't know what held me together emotionally for another week, but Xara persuaded me to return to that horrid class with her. This time it seemed different, as though the message was meant for me.

Mrs. Cooper said that God had a design for *my* life. He loved *me,* she said, but the reason I wasn't experiencing the abundant life He wanted me to have was because I was sinful, and sin separates us from God. Jesus, however, came to bridge the gap between humans and God. Alone, I could never be good enough for God, but God had given His perfect Son, who took the judgment for *my* sin when He died on the cross. It was a *personal* thing. I could accept Him as my Saviour, a transaction between Jesus Christ and Anne. I, Anne, could have a one-to-one, fulfilling relationship with the Son of God!

Excitement ran through me. I understood for the first time that my belief in Jesus had been only an intellectual acknowledgement of His existence. *I had not trusted Jesus Christ to make me acceptable to God,* as He offered to do.

I had always thought of the death of Christ as a mass project ("Christ died for the world"), but now I saw that if I had been the only person in the world, Jesus still would have come and died for *me* . . . Anne . . . to reconcile me to God!

It was instant identity, a beautiful self-image. God loves me!

Now I knew what I had spent all those years searching for. I was 28, and I had found the One who could be the solution to all my problems!

I must have hit Jim with all my new enthusiasm like a loaded freight train. With a taste of what Christ could mean to our lives, I proceeded to stuff salvation down Jim's throat. I preached day and night, too busy giving out my unseasoned truth to him to learn any more for myself, let alone apply it to my life.

God said, "My thoughts are not your thoughts, neither are your ways my ways (Isa. 55:8). I didn't realize that, nor did I understand what it meant to "wait on the Lord." I ran full-steam ahead, trying to drag Christ along, to make Him fit into my plans. I'm sure He tried to slow me down a few times, but I was running too fast to hear.

In the summer I spent a week at a Bible conference and came home brimming with spiritual energy—to find Jim gone! When he finally got in, it was obvious he hadn't been pining away for me. Still I didn't catch on that I was asking him to compete with Jesus Christ. I wasn't the girl Jim married, nor was I yet the woman Christ was trying to design. But on I rushed.

I had clear notions about how I should look, act, and dress. Single handedly, I hoped to convert the world. It would be nice to have Jim's approval, but it seemed more important that he please me and further my ministry. By Christmas time I was about to blossom into full sainthood and ascend Mt. Sinai to receive a second set of Commandments. At that point Jim decided he'd had it with his live-in "Billy Graham" —he asked for a divorce.

I couldn't believe it. To some people looking on, it seemed that Jim was all wrong and I was altogether right. For a while it seemed like that to me, too.

But Jesus Christ had something to teach me through the alienation. God waited patiently while I retraveled the singles route and discovered the pastures none too green. Meanwhile my deep love for Jim persisted. Tired and disgusted, feeling I'd done all I should and still failed, I cried, "My God, I've tried everything. I quit."

It was as if He said, "Great. Now, Anne, I can get to work."

By this time, Darien and I were close friends. I spent many hours seeking her counsel and her knowledge of the Bible. She was so patient through those difficult times. I'm sure she became weary at times when I'd talk out the same problem for the tenth time, or ask for an explanation of principles we'd gone over many times before. Sometimes I felt as if the Lord were using me to give Darien counseling practice for her course, "Will the Real Woman Please Stand Up?"

The first principle we worked on was my acceptance of Jim. I recognized that I had used many ways to let Jim know I wanted him to be different. But Jesus hadn't demanded that of me. Although Jim and I were now divorced, we saw one another frequently. I started to accept Jim just as he was, with no hope of his changing.

As the Bible principles took shape in my life, I learned that God is the Father who never lets me down. Repeatedly my experiences strengthened my sense of being worthwhile and very special to God.

As I obeyed Him, Jesus rekindled the fires of devotion between Jim and me. Better than that, we developed a deeper, more precious relationship. Two and a half years after our divorce, Jim asked me again to become his wife! I wrote the thoughts and words of our love into the wedding ceremony which reunited us.

Working out our new relationship was a gradual yet exciting process. With my acceptance of Jim, I learned to give my expectations to the Lord. The psalmist wrote: "Delight yourself also in the Lord, and He will give you the desires *and* secret petitions of your heart. Commit your way unto the Lord—roll and repose [each care of] your road on Him; trust . . . also in Him, and He will bring it to pass" (Ps. 37:4-5, AMP.).

I tried to keep these verses constantly before me. I stopped asking him where he was going, unless I needed it as business information. Whenever he showed up, I let him know I was glad to see him. No more pouting fits or complaints marred his ties at home. He spent more and more time with me. Often now, Jim comes home sooner than he's planned. I guess home is a nicer place to come back to, today.

My goodie-goodie image had to go. Owing to my preconceived ideas of Christian behavior, I had been very careful about where I was seen. And I had changed from really swinging fashions to things that made me look like Granny Grunch. My self-righteous attitudes and actions made for a Madonna complex, and I learned that no man can relate to a Madonna. As part of making amends, I told Jim I would wear whatever he liked. He tested me for a short time, but when he saw that I really did it to please him, we agreed on fashions that we both enjoy.

Part of the principle of letting him lead the family helps me as much as it does Jim. He had been used to my handling things like any business*man,* but I learned to let him handle even some small things. For instance, when I was harassed by a collector for a newspaper bill we didn't owe, I told the man that he would have to come back when my husband was home. When I told Jim, he called the person responsible and told him not to send anyone again to his home and insult his wife. Now when I'm asked to make a decision when Jim is not around, I say, "I'm sorry. You'll have to talk to my husband about that." Of course, Jim knows I will take care of anything he delegates to me, but he tries to keep undue pressure off me.

Following the leader works in three specific changes that I made in my approach to problems: I now leave the preaching to preachers; I share my opinions with Jim, but leave the final decision to him; and I give him responsibility for the rules and discipline of our children. I have learned to relax and enjoy the protection of my husband's leadership.

I don't mean to imply we are without problems, for who is? When I think of Jim's and my relationship, I am reminded of Song of Solomon 8:7, "Many waters cannot quench love, neither can floods drown it," and 1 Corinthians 13:8, "Love never fails—never fades out or becomes obsolete or comes to an end" (AMP). These things speak to me of the permanence which God intended for love. I wouldn't take anything for our having struggled through the bad years. I love Jim more than words could ever express, and I thank the Lord for reuniting us because truly now, "My beloved is mine, and I am his" (Song 2:16).

Jim has done a lot of maturing. His devil-may-care air is mellowing with an underlying strength. A real warmth and concern for others are emerging elements of a beautiful new personality. His faith is still a private matter between him and God, kept close to his heart with the other profoundly personal subjects nourished in his individualism.

When I revert to seeing things from a human viewpoint, Christ gently corrects me; it's as if He says, "Anne, you've taken your eyes from Me and you're looking at the world and at yourself." I remember that He is painting the picture of my life, and He sees the full image. Then I affirm that when Jesus is in control of my life He is responsible for "working all things to our good."

When my faith wavers, I remember what a bomb I made out of my life, and how looking through His eyes changed a hopeless situation into a bright beginning.

Jesus is my constant companion and friend. I talk to Him continually. "Look at this," I say. "Isn't this fantastic!" Or, "What should I do now, Lord? I know You want the best for me; don't let me goof." I may need to confess: "Lord, I sinned, I've fallen short. But I know You can work it out for my good. Lord, it is so comforting to know You love me more than I love myself, and you love Jim even more than I do, and Lord, I just thank You for being with us, for loving us. Thank You, Lord."

Jesus loves me even when I'm unlovable. That's what I needed to know in order to live and to journey back to love.

Reminiscing With Darien:

The neighborhood Bible class seemed like any other on that wintry Wednesday morning except for the very stylish, sophisticated young woman sitting on the front row. Later I learned her name was Anne Carroll. I wondered about her, "Why did she come? What did she hope to find, and would she return?"

She continued to come each week and gradually began staying longer and longer after the classes to talk with me. At first, she seemed so knowledgeable on every subject that I wondered if I dared reveal how uninformed I was about the things of the world she was discussing. My newly learned truth of simply being myself—open and honest with no pretense—was challenged. I wanted her to respect and like me. Could I risk losing it? Yes, God was teaching me that as long as I had His approval, He would draw to me needed and dear friends (Prov. 3:1-16).

Only God could have brought together two people so opposite in background and personality to teach each so very much and to establish such a beautiful friendship.

Periodic phone conversations soon became a daily occurrence. I began to learn through our relationship what had only been a theory before: regardless of the mask we wear or the impression we give to others of ourselves, we are *all* alike on the inside. Anne had searched from early teens to find peace and fulfillment as a person. So had I. While I had not been able to hide my feelings of inferiority, she had covered hers deftly with a mask of "Miss Self-Sufficiency." But her disguise hadn't helped any more than my admitted inadequacy.

Blaise Pascal, physicist and philosopher, identified this universal need when he said, "There is a God-shaped vacuum in the heart of each man which cannot be satisfied by any created thing, but only by God, the Creator, made known through Jesus Christ."

It was exciting to watch the reversal in Anne's thinking as

she started seeing herself as God saw her, a person of tremendous worth. Since the value of anything may be judged by the price placed on it, she saw that she was infinitely precious since the life of Jesus Christ, infinite payment, had been given for her. Not only did accepting the death of the Son of God for herself give Anne the right to fellowship with God, but God also declared that He was *richer* by her receiving His Son as her Saviour (Eph. 1:8). Anne gained comfort from God's *unconditional acceptance* of her in Christ and at last she began to experience fellowship with God through the Saviour.

As Anne's relationship with God deepened, she learned to deal with others in proper perspective. God said she was His *ambassador* (2 Cor. 55:20); she had no need to worry, because God promised to *meet all of her needs*—personal and marital (Phil. 4:19). These needs were met through our searching the Scriptures together and applying the answers we found there.

As Anne began to see herself from God's perspective, her direct, almost abrupt manner began to soften, and her tender, caring nature began to be manifested. By becoming God-centered, the identity crisis was over and she was well on her way to becoming the "divine original" that God had created her to be.

Perhaps you have some of Anne's problems. Or maybe you'd profit by the self-evaluation and Bible study afforded in the following questions and Scripture passages.

Thinking Through With You:

Question: *What kind of life does God desire for us?*
Answer: "I have told you these things that My joy *and* delight may be in you, and that your joy *and* gladness may be full measure *and* complete *and* overflowing" (John 15:11, AMP.).

Q.: *What separates us from God's approval and blessings?*
A.: "Your iniquities have made a separation between you and your God, and your sins have hid His face from you, so that He will not hear" (Isaiah 59:2, AMP.).

Q.: *How can we get rid of these sins?*
A.: "God caused Christ, who Himself knew nothing of sin, actually to *be* sin for our sakes, so that in Christ we might be made good with the goodness of God" (2 Corinthians 5:21, PH). "Who [Christ] personally in His own body carried our sins onto the cross, so that we might abandon our sins and live for righteousness" (1 Peter 2:24, BERK).

What remains for us to do?

"Believe in the Lord Jesus and then you will be saved" (Acts 16:31, PH). "In view of God's mercies, that you present your bodies a living sacrifice . . . to God . . . And do not conform to the present world scheme, but be transformed by a complete renewal of mind, so as to sense for yourselves what is the good and acceptable and perfect will of God" (Rom. 12:1-2, BERK).

2

God Didn't Take
Over Until I Let Go!

Bonnie West

With mixed feelings, I joined my friends in the waiting car. We were going to hear Darien Cooper teach "Will the Real Woman Please Stand Up?" I was excited because I loved to hear the Bible explained, but I was apprehensive because I didn't want to receive a set of rules to follow. And I hated to take study notes.

Worse yet, I had heard that the course would teach me submission to my husband. I had carefully circumvented that Bible concept. The Scripture phrase "as unto the Lord" seemed too deep for me. Recently, however, I had decided to let Christ have full control of my life, and I thought there *might* be something in the course to help me with my problems.

I had grown up not knowing my father, as he died when I was a baby. Out of necessity, my mother made a place for herself in the business world of our small, typically Southern town. She was independent and quite capable in her real estate field. I deeply admired her. There was one thing, however, I wished she had time to do. In my daydreams I envisioned her wearing an apron and humming while working over a warm stove baking a cake. But since she had to be the family breadwinner there seemed no time to bake cakes.

In spite of that, we lived a satisfying life. We went to a church where, at nine, I accepted Jesus Christ as my personal Saviour. Mother and I shared many friends in common. Our closest companions were our neighbors, who were mostly widows.

We had no close relatives living nearby and there was little chance for me to observe a husband-and-wife relationship. For a reason I didn't understand at the time, I found playing with my school friends to be an unsettling experience when their fathers came home. I would leave immediately—even when the mother was humming and lovingly baking a cake! Now I realize that, not having a father, I was insecure in this unfamiliar relationship. Since I had little idea what marriage was supposed to be like, I concluded that I was to be just like my mother: self-sufficient.

Mike and I had our first argument on our honeymoon trip. I wanted to purchase a dog and take him several hundred miles back home with us. Mike suggested we wait until we got home to buy a pet. I insisted we do it my way; he decided we would do it his way—and he drove past the pet shop. Consequently we rode 500 miles in frigid silence, while I wondered what I had got myself into!

We discovered that our interests went in opposite directions. I loved libraries and reading. I even tried to write for magazines. A romantic at heart, I was also definitely the indoor type. Mike's world seemed to revolve around football and basketball games, mostly on television.

I learned to loosen some tubes in the television set when a "big game" was coming up—there was a big one every week! But Mike soon figured out that I had been tampering with the TV, and he readily fixed it while I crept away to sulk.

Mike was meticulous, always checking on details. I ignored them and worked out my own way to do things. It seemed Mike never, *never* got in a hurry, and I was always ready for things ahead of time. Mike thrived on talking with strangers at a gathering, while I couldn't think of a thing to say. He stayed up late; I went to bed early. He relished traveling and I preferred staying home. The clincher was that Mike liked to eat—and I hated to cook!

Four children certainly gave us something in common, but we argued about discipline and my having to care for them. Some days I imagined myself running away and leaving Mike with the kids for a while—until he would welcome me back with due appreciation!

I finally admitted that there must be a better way to live than the one Mike and I were following. That's when I heard my friends talking about "Will the Real Woman Please Stand Up?" They said 500 or more women attended each seminar. I understood that the principles taught there helped a wife to become what her husband wanted her to be. If that were true, it seemed to be just what I needed, because I felt that I wasn't anything like what Mike wanted.

As I sat waiting for the class to begin, I looked around at the other women. I wondered if my problems were like theirs, or worse. Then Darien arrived, and as soon as she started talking everyone began taking notes. Even though I knew I'd lose mine, or couldn't understand them when I got home, I pulled out my pen and scribbled away.

Suddenly I felt as if Darien were talking about me—just me—and I looked around to see if anyone was staring at me. But, of course, no one was. Then I became so fascinated with what she was saying that I put down my pen and just listened.

God works through the husband for the benefit of the wife, she said. When the wife understands and believes this, she can trust God in any situation. She is released from the pressure of trying to change her husband, of manipulating him into doing what she wants. Favorable results are then produced by lovingly responding to her husband's leadership and leaving the results to God.

Realizing Christ accepts her just as she is, a wife can then thank God for her husband *just as he is*. If he asks her to do something she isn't interested in or hasn't the appitude for, she can do it lovingly, recalling the verse which says "Wives, be subject—be submissive and adapt yourselves—to your own husbands as [a service] to the Lord" (Eph 5:22, AMP). An "I'll-do-it-even-if-it-kills-me" attitude isn't the same thing!

Darien read Scripture verses to underscore the principles she was sharing. She stressed that she wasn't talking about the wife as a namby-pamby doormat. God gave us our own beautiful individuality; God created the wife to be a helpmate for her husband—a complement to him.

The idea that God would work His will for my life through my husband entranced me. I went away from the class with the idea boldly in front of me, like a giant billboard.

I began applying some of the practical principles Darien had suggested. I didn't complain when Mike went to play golf, or when he tracked mud into the house, or when he isolated himself behind the sports page. He began watching me with suspicion. One day he acknowledged my new attitude with, "What's happened to you? Why don't we fuss anymore?"

As the class continued to meet, I began to realize that I had been asuming a lot of responsiblilities that weren't mine. For instance, I thought it extravagant for Mike to buy new tires for the cars while the old ones were still rolling. Consequently, when he announced, "I bought two new tires for your car today," he knew what to expect: I would name all the things I could have bought with that tire money, and I'd tell him I didn't want to hear about treads. Now I realized that the care of the cars is Mike's responsibility. Like a wet puppy shaking itself, I shook myself free of his responsibility.

The next time he said, "I got you a new tire today," I replied, "Thank you." Then I went out to look at it on the car. I told him, "You picked out a lovely tire." He chuckled, and I grinned. There was appreciation for me beneath his laughter.

But there were times when I didn't manage so well. There was the day Mike told me about the rotten tomato in the refrigerator just after I had (1) waxed the kitchen floor,

(2) scrubbed the cabinets, and (3) cooked his favorite supper. Feeling very unappreciated, my human nature took over and I wouldn't have removed that moldy old tomato or apologized for anything!

Generally, though, I began reacting differently about the things I'd wanted my way for years. While listening to Darien during one of the class sessions, I began thinking, "Surely God doesn't want me to like football for Mike's sake—not that!" Just at that moment Darien said, "If your husband is a football nut and wants you to enjoy the games with him, ask Jesus to take over. He will."

On the way home that day, I asked God to help me "endure football." Then I changed it to "like football." And I added, "I'm trusting You to do this for me."

Sure enough, within a few days, Mike asked me to go with him later in the season to a football game. I heard myself answer "yes" in a small but animated voice.

I had never seen him so excited. For two months he talked about the game we were going to "together." As for me, I felt no bitterness or resentment, though I didn't share the same degree of anticipation.

The sun shone warmly as we walked into the stadium that December afternoon. Mike explained some of the more exciting plays and I actually began to understand some. Sitting with Mike in the midst of thousands of screaming fans, I looked up at the bright blue sky and thought, "You really take over when we let you, Lord. Thank You."

It didn't occur to me right away that Mike had acted differently by planning so far ahead. I am the one who loves to plan things months in advance and scrawl the upcoming events on my calendar. Mike likes to play things by ear and "hang loose." Consequently it was hard for me to let go of a problem and trust God to work through my husband when I had to wait so long for Mike's decisions.

Waiting is hard for me. I tend to work out solutions and pray, "God, this is ready for Your blessing. Isn't it a terrific idea!" Of course, I may disguise my prayer in pretty language, using "Your will" or "make me teachable," but often the attitude of my heart is "Let's get going, God."

Mike and I had been married nearly 17 years and the Lord was doing so many exciting things in my life and my marriage that I wanted to write about them. Writing was a dream come true for me. Within a few months' time my articles had been accepted by several magazines. Then, after praying about it, I began rewriting a book which I had started four years earlier.

Since Mike objected to my writing when he was home, I stopped whenever I heard his car in the driveway. I also tried to have supper ready in the evenings and to keep the house looking fairly neat.

But one morning with the writing going great, I didn't stop for eight hours straight. I paid no attention to the house, the children, the telephone, supper, nor to Mike when he drove up. I heedlessly kept on typing. Obviously, my priorities were out of order.

When Mike entered the house, he saw I was exhausted. He said I had no right to drive myself so hard and to ignore the children and our home. An argument ensued and Mike picked up the manuscript and threw it across the floor. His contempt seemed almost as horrible to me as if he had swung violently at one of our children!

I ran upstairs and slumped to my knees. Sobbing to my Father in heaven, I asked Him to help me give up the book if Mike didn't want me to write it.

When I went downstairs, Mike apologized. He didn't beat around the bush, either. He said the words, "I'm sorry." Then he told me to go ahead with the book. He was concerned, however, for my physical and mental well being. So I tried to work less frantically.

When the book was finished, I asked Mike to read what I had written, because it was about us. I wanted his approval before I sent it to a publisher.

Mike didn't get around to reading it for two weeks. In his spare time he watched television and read the papers. Inside

I was screaming, "Read it, read it, you stubborn man! Why don't you read it?" Then another thought whispered through my mind, "Trust God. Be patient."

I mourned in silent anguish as Mike enjoyed television. When I could stand it no longer, I tried asking him again to read it. He replied that he'd get around to it. I felt as if I were being torn apart inside. I kept telling myself I was trusting God to work through Mike, though I wasn't.

Finally Mike started reading. Ever so slowly, it seemed to me, he perused it. One day he said it would be all right to mail.

I was at the post office within the hour.

But serious damage had been done. A few days later I awoke with pains in my chest. The spasms grew to an unbearable intensity. I was hospitalized with one of the largest stomach ulcers my doctor had ever seen. I knew immediately that my impatience and lack of trust had caused it. My first reaction was, "Oh, I don't want God to know about this ulcer. I'm so ashamed."

I believe God had to teach me this lesson the hard way: the danger of trying to make a drastic change in behavior on my own. I realized that Christ can do things—change us and others—only when we totally let go. Trusting isn't saying, "It's Yours, Lord," and then thinking behind His back you can continue to apply your own solutions. You'll never find the quote, "God helps those who help themselves," in the Bible.

I bowed my head and prayed for forgiveness. Then I asked God to heal the ulcer. I wanted no reminder of my disobedient attitude. Within six weeks the ulcer vanished without a trace. The doctor even allowed me to resume following a normal diet.

When I truly give a problem to God—completely let go of it—it is amazing how He takes over. Our pastor approached me one day to ask if Mike and I could attend a "lay renewal weekend" coming up in a couple of months. My answer surprised me, and the pastor mirrored my astonishment. I said, "I'll tell Mike about it, and whatever *he* says, we'll do."

Normally I would have tried to push Mike into anything I wanted to do. Demand an answer from him. Make him commit himself. Put it on my calendar. So a part of me wanted to insist: *get an answer from Mike tonight.* But, against my nature, I gave the matter to the Lord. Even though I wanted terribly to go, I trusted God to work through my husband for our good.

When I told Mike, he replied right away. "We can't go." Then he paused as if waiting for my rebuttal.

"OK," I said with a smile. It wasn't a gushy response. Nor was it a martyred, goody-two-shoes attitude. The desire to attend left me completely and I was somehow glad we weren't going!

A couple of days later Mike asked me what time he'd need to get off work in order for us to attend the first session of the conference, if we went. We had not been away for a weekend, just the two of us, in years. Planning for the care of four children would be a problem, and it was a bad time for Mike to get away from the office. I realized that Mike was reasonably and responsibly weighing his decision.

Weeks slipped by and the pastor needed a definite yes or no. I put the question to Mike. "Is it all right to tell him we can't go?"

"No, we're going."

"Really!" I squealed. My desire to go returned and intensified in a split second.

Then it hit me! I hadn't suffered while waiting for Mike to make up his mind—I had been trusting Christ to do what was best for us. Those dates on my calendar remained blank all that time, and it didn't matter in the least!

I thank God that each day gives me new chances to be Mike's helpmate. I've relinquished many "'rights" from my grasp and since I opened my fist I've discovered that Mike wants to hold my hand!

Reminiscing with Darien:

Ring-ring-ring. The telephone interrupted my thoughts as I sat at the kitchen table writing.

"Hello."

"My name is Bonnie West. I attended your spring class entitled, 'Will the Real Woman Please Stand Up?' Since I did not get to meet you at that time, I wanted to share with you some of the things I am seeing God do in my life."

Bonnie's enthusiasm over the biblical truths God was teaching her was not minimized by the miles of telephone line. I could immediately identify with her excitement. God had begun teaching me those same truths a few years ago.

Such an interruption of my writing was truly welcome. Getting to know Bonnie as we talked about the reality of Jesus Christ in our everyday living was very rewarding to me.

Bonnie became a Christian as a child, but had not learned how to live the Christian life. She was discovering that the Christian life is not only difficult to live but is impossible— by oneself! Only Jesus Christ can live such a life. Not only had Christ died to pay for Bonnie's sins, but He rose again to relive His life in and through her, moment by moment.

Bonnie realized that such power had not been a reality in her life for two reasons. First, she was unaware of the provision God had made for her as His child. She was living in spiritual poverty when God had provided an abundance. Her condition could be compared to having a million dollars in her bank account while living in poverty, unaware of her wealth.

Second, God's power had been limited in her life because of unconfessed sin. Bonnie learned that worry, jealousy, a critical attitude, bitterness, revenge, self-pity (to name a few) were symptoms of self rather than Christ being in control. The Holy Spirit was grieved by these sins. The moment she confessed her sins, claiming the promise in 1 John 1:9, she was cleansed and again controlled by the Holy Spirit as she yielded to Him.

Even though confessing one's sins is imperative in the Christian life, confession is not enough to break the old habit patterns. For instance, if you found a beetle on his back kicking his feet in the air, you might conclude that his problem would be corrected by placing him on his feet. After doing so, you observe that he starts back up the same incline that caused his fall. Then you realize that he needs to be headed in another direction. Likewise, we must begin to respond to our husbands, children, in-laws, and others as God instructs, as well as ceasing harmful actions.

Bonnie began to realize that her relationship to Mike was to have the same ingredients as her relationship with Jesus Christ. At first she was frightened to accept Mike exactly as he was. Wouldn't he take advantage of her and start doing everything "wrong" if he knew she'd respond lovingly, regardless? Then she remembered that she didn't respond spitefully to Christ when she learned He loved her equally at all times. She had been drawn to Him, desiring to be all that He wanted her to be.

Bonnie realized that acceptance of Mike must not be conditional. She was to respect his God-given right to make his own decisions without coercion from her or being penalized by her if he didn't do what she had desired. Such acceptance provides the atmosphere necessary to bring out the best in a person. Mike immediately began to respond, showing appreciation and admiration for the sweet spirit she displayed. Other men may test their wives to see if their acceptance is genuine or just a new gimmick to get their own way. But Christian wives can have perfect peace, knowing that this is God's way for them to respond. After all, the wife is responsible only for herself, not for her husband.

Accepting your husband as he is provides a basis for his dignity as a person. A man's self-esteem can be undermined when you attempt to coerce, set limits, or put conditions on what he does. He may react by withdrawing into himself, becoming passive and suffer in an attempt to keep a peaceful attitude. Outwardly he turns into a "mouse." Or he may rebel against the restraints and resemble a roaring "lion" around the house. Either way, the traits are hard to respect in a man. But manly qualities require the self-esteem you can help build in your husband.

God never asks you to accept your husband or fulfill any other request in the Christian life without providing the means whereby His will can be accomplished. Philippians 4:6-9 gives the formula for responding properly to problems —marital or otherwise.

The first step is to give your problem to God: "Be anxious for nothing, but in everything, by prayer and supplication, with thanksgiving, let your requests be made known to God" (Phil. 4:6, NASB).

Bonnie faced the fact that even though God's way is not always easy, it is easier than doing things her way. She began to consistently place marital problems into God's hands. When the problems entered her thinking, she simply said, "Thank You, Lord, that You are handling that problem. It's going to be exciting to see how You work it out."

Once God has been given access to our problems, the next step is to cooperate with Him as He works out the solution. Verse eight describes this: "Whatever is true, whatever is honorable, whatever is right, whatever is pure, whatever is lovely, whatever is of good repute, if there is any excellence and if anything worthy of praise, let your mind dwell on these things" (Phil. 4:8, NASB).

God's way of working out problems varies. He enabled Bonnie to enjoy the football game rather than taking away Mike's yen for sports. But He led Mike to approve her desire to write. Bonnie learned from their argument that her priorities should be as follows: (1) maintaining her relationship with Jesus Christ through Bible study and prayer, (2) being her husband's help-mate, (3) caring for their children's needs, (4) caring for her personal needs—diet, exercise, rest, and appearance. (5) housekeeping responsibilities, and (6) personal hobbies and activities. With her priorities in order, Bonnie's writing enhanced rather than destroyed precious relationships.

Verse 9 of Philippians 4 is important to remember also. "Practice these things" (NASB). Some days the spiritually sensitive wife may feel that all she does is confess her sins, give problems to God, and focus on positive truths. But as we are obedient each time to these directions, we find ourselves experiencing God's peace more and more.

Thinking Through with You

Question: *How is the Christian life lived successfully?*
Answer: "I have been crucified with Christ and I no longer live, but Christ lives in me. The life I live in the body, I live by faith in the Son of God, who loved me and gave Himself for me" (Gal. 2:20, NIV).

Q.: *What kinds of qualities will be manifested in my life when I am under Christ's control?*
A.: "The fruit of the Spirit is love, joy, peace, patience, kindness, goodness, faithfulness, gentleness, self control" (Gal. 5:22-23, NASB).

Q.: *If insisting on my rights involves constantly checking on my husband, expecting him to share every thought and move, demanding meal attendance at my time and convenience, and criticizing his failures, what does love involve?*
A.: "Love is patient, love is kind. It does not envy, it does not boast, it is not proud. It is not rude, it is not self-seeking, it is not easily angered, it keeps no record of wrongs. Love does not delight in evil but rejoices in the truth. It always protects, always trusts, always hopes, always perseveres" (1 Cor 13:4-7, NIV).

Q.: *What relieves you of the responsibility and burden of changing your husband?*
A.: "Each of us will give an account of himself to God" (Rom. 14:12, NIV).

Q.: *What can you expect from God if you take your problems to Him in prayer and thank Him for taking over?*
A.: "The peace of God, which surpasses all comprehension, shall guard your hearts and your minds in Christ Jesus" (Phil. 4:7, NASB).

3

The Fans Are Silent
But My Praises Ring

Chris Sorpenski

Cool breezes blew off the bay and the California sun cast giant shadows across the football field as the 49ers ran on for the last game of the season. Fans slowly filled Kezar Stadium. Taking my regular seat, I wondered if Dusty and I would miss the glamor and glory of the past years. Would anything else match the roar of the crowd, instant recognition at restaurants, and the advantages of being a professional football player?

Waiting for the game to start, I thought back to the first time I met Dusty. After my parents divorced, I had lived with my grandparents in Carmel. It was at a charity bazaar one summer afternoon that I had first seen Dusty. After graduating from Stanford University in the spring, my summer had been filled with parties and trips. Only at the last moment had I decided to go to the bazaar.

After greeting my hostess, I talked with many of the girls that I had grown up with. Much time was spent in "catch-up" conversation. Grandfather had brought me and he was insistent that I meet some of the young men.

Dusty was one of them. I was instantly taken with him, but his name, Duston Sorpenski, was a bit much. As we talked, I learned he had recently graduated from Ohio State and had come to San Francisco to play professional football.

A few weeks later, Dusty called and asked me to go to a party given by one of the rookies. After the party we drove back up the coast to Carmel. There we stopped the car and sat on a ridge overlooking the Pacific. A gnarled old tree stood on the edge of the cliff, twisted by the constant ocean winds. Looking at Dusty, I thought, "I could stand up through the storms of life just like that old tree if I had this man beside me."

When Dusty proposed marriage a few months later, I was thrilled. I felt that he was the greatest thing that could ever happen to me. He was so tall, dark, and handsome. He was sweet, patient, loving, kind, and a truly gentle man. Being a professional athlete, he had a marvelous physique. When I fell in love with Dusty, I fell so hard that I thought I loved him as much as it was humanly possible to love anyone.

After becoming a Christian at the age of 12, I had not made Jesus a prominent part of my life. But as I approached marriage I became aware of this lack. I spoke with our minister, and the morning of our wedding I reaffirmed my commitment to Christ. Dusty and I had briefly discussed Christianity. He told me that he, too, came to know Christ at an early age. I wanted a Christian marriage, with never any thought of divorce. I wanted our future children to have a happy home and the family togetherness that I never had.

After Dusty and I were married, we faithfully attended church each Sunday, but our spiritual training began and ended there. After two years of marriage, the Lord gave us a beautiful baby girl, and we were thrilled. Three years passed, and we were again blessed with a precious baby boy. Our family was now complete. We loved our children dearly and sincerely wanted to raise them in the ways of the Lord.

As soon as they were old enough, we started them in Sunday School. They were taught to ask the blessing before meals and to pray before going to bed. Bible stories were taught to them, but I now know that Jesus was not vital in any of our lives. We never mentioned Christ in ordinary conversation.

We realized the lack of Christian instruction one Christmas when our daughter Oma confused Jesus with Santa Claus. I wanted Christ's birthday to be meaningful to our children, so I went out and bought a manger scene. We shared with the children the real meaning of Christmas. I realized then that all of us needed more than a manger scene could give, but pride still dominated my personality.

Dusty's decision to retire from football was going to bring a great change in my life. I had spent all my years in California, and now for the first time I would be moving away.

I knew Dusty felt that time was catching up with him. Almost ten years as a professional football player was more than most players could expect. But giving up the "good life" in California was not going to be easy for either of us.

The throbbing notes of the National Anthem broke through my thoughts and returned me to the reality of the moment. I watched the players run out on the field and listened to their names being announced. "Number 63, center, Duston Sorpenski." Tears welled up in my eyes as I realized this was the last time I would hear that announcement. The game itself became something of a blur in my memory.

Dusty had bought a large motor-hotel in Gatlinburg, Tennessee. We were going into a new business, in a totally different part of the country. Since Gatlinburg is basically a resort town at the western entrance to the Smoky Mountains, we had decided to make our permanent home in Atlanta, Georgia.

The children glowed expectantly as they watched the movers place the last piece of furniture in the van. It was warm as we left Carmel in mid-February. Arriving in Atlanta, we found the ground, trees, and telephone wires weighted down with ice. Like a Disneyland fantasy, the whole city seemed to be frozen. I longingly thought of the warm California sun.

After a few weeks of eight- and nine-hour days with a patient real estate agent, we found a lovely home in the Indian

Hills section. The children adjusted quickly to their new schools and friends, and life went on as usual.

Dusty spent a lot of time in Gatlinburg, getting the motel ready for the tourist season. There was much work to be done. The rooms needed remodeling, new furniture was being delivered, and menus had to be planned for the motel restaurant.

I met wonderful new friends. Much time was spent decorating our new home. As spring came to Atlanta, I was astounded by the beauty of the dogwoods and azaleas. Memories of California quickly faded from my mind.

Spring turned into fall and again into spring. And the steady strains of business, life, and marriage began to bear down on us.

I had always considered myself a good woman. I thought I was a good Christian, a good friend, a good wife, and good mother. But if I had been entirely truthful as far as my marriage was concerned, I would have admitted I was a domineering, possessive, stubborn, demanding, and immature partner.

One of our periodic hangups arose when Dusty and I had a disagreement and I would insist that it be settled before we went to sleep. "It just isn't right to go to sleep with this strain between us," I would cry.

"Chris, don't you realize it's 3 o'clock in the morning?" His voice was taut, disgusted. "Let's talk about it tomorrow. I'm tired."

But I could never let it drop.

And I usually wanted my own way. One evening Dusty came home and said, "Hey, Chris, why don't you fix a quick dinner for the kids and let's us go out?"

"Fantastic!" I said, and began making sandwiches. "Where are we going?"

"Oh, I thought we'd go to Aunt Fanny's. I've had my mouth set all day for some of that country ham."

"Really, Dusty . . . not Aunt Fanny's. I'm in the mood for violins and the Midnight Sun."

"You have got to be kidding," he said. "I don't want to

get dressed up and I don't want to drive that far. I just want ham."

"Well, I don't, and if we can't go to the Midnight Sun I don't want to go out at all!"

The rest of the evening simmered in silence, with Dusty watching TV and me pouting in the bedroom.

Sometimes I was downright irrational. For Christmas one year, I got Dusty a beautiful Browning 300 magnum rifle. I had asked one of his friends to go with me to pick it out, since I didn't know much about guns, and I wanted it to be just what he wanted.

The problem arose when Dusty wanted to use the beautiful equipment I had given him—a hunting trip was planned or a fishing trip was in the offing. I would pout and cry because I didn't want Dusty to go! I wanted Dusty to have all that gear but I didn't want him to enjoy activities which excluded me.

Possessiveness wasn't all that plagued me. Resentment and a profound feeling of not being wanted filled my being at times. Once upset, I turned skirmishes into drawn-out battles. It took days and even weeks to get over my horrible feelings of the hurt and malice. Dusty could explode one moment and in the next be happy and loving. Not me! He would apologize repeatedly, whether he was right or wrong.

"Chris," he'd say, "I'm sorry; I didn't realize that I had upset you so."

"It just doesn't matter," I'd reply. "You wouldn't have acted like that if you loved me."

"Chris, I do love you. You're just impossible at times."

"See, you said it again. You don't love me!" Like a child denied candy, I'd pooch out my lip and stomp out of the room.

There were many happy times, of course, and for the most part people thought we were an ideal couple. And as long as things were going my way, peace prevailed.

Early one spring a horrible argument boiled up. Dusty told me he was going to Gatlinberg to prepare the motel for the coming season. He had never gone this early before, and I was dead-set against it.

He said, "Chris, don't you understand? The rooms need painting, the gutters need cleaning, and you know if I'm not there the work won't get done."

"We've got a manager to oversee things like that," I protested. "I can see no good reason for you to go right now. This is two weeks earlier than you've ever gone before."

"Well, if you can't understand, I'm not going to stand here all night trying to explain it to you," he said, and walked into the bedroom.

I wasn't going to let him get away with that. If it took all night, I was going to get things settled—my way.

Walking into the bedroom, I said, "Dusty, we're not going to drop it just like that."

"Yes, I am," he said. He walked out into the hall to pick up some business papers, and I followed him, fussing with every step.

He went back into the bedroom and shut and locked the door. Obviously, he had had enough for the evening. Knowing that I wasn't about to drop the subject, he tried to retreat and find some solitude.

Totally enraged, I screamed and hollered, beating on the bedroom door. Knowing I would wake everyone in the house, he furiously jerked open the door, grabbed my arm and pulled me in.

When he let go, I was off balance and stumbled and fell into an end table. A crystal vase fell as I upset the table and broke under my arm as it hit the floor. With blood dripping from the cut on my arm, I walked pathetically into the bathroom.

The accident ended our conversation that night. But the next morning I found Dusty had packed his bags and left. I wasn't sure whether he had left me or had just gone to Gatlinburg.

I realized that if he hadn't left me for good, it might not be long until he did. I prayed that the Lord would help me and help our marriage. I knew I was destroying it, but I didn't have the slightest idea how to begin to make changes.

My Sunday School teacher had often asked me to attend a Bible class which met every other week. Needing help so very much, I decided to go. One day at Bible study, someone was reading Ephesions 5. When she read verse 24, "Now as the church submits to Christ, so also wives should submit to their husbands in everything" (NIV). I immediately asked the group if they *really* obeyed their husbands. There was a moment of silence, and then one of them asked me if the word "obey" was in my marriage vows. I quickly said yes, but I sat there thinking that obeying my husband would be the last thing I would do.

It is ironical that the minister who married us referred us to Ephesians 5 as an important chapter for marriage, and yet I had never applied it to mine.

A few months later when I was discussing a current book on marriage with a friend, she asked me if I had read *You Can Be The Wife Of A Happy Husband*. She let me borrow her copy and I began reading the Christian principles and truths taught by Darien Cooper. I realized what kind of wife God expects a Christian woman to be and I saw how far short I fell.

The Lord began to counsel me about not being possessive, demanding, domineering, and holding resentments. As I was responsive, Christ began to change me. When I heard that Mrs. Cooper would be teaching a seminar on the book topic, a friend and I began to attend.

When we arrived at the first class, Anne Carroll was speaking. I was fascinated with her story and was encouraged to see the transformation the Lord had performed in her life. I knew then that no matter how strained my relationship with Dusty had become, Christ could make the necessary changes if I made myself totally available to Him and applied His principles for a Christian marriage.

After listening to Mrs. Cooper, I became aware of the necessity of obeying God's Word. I developed a hunger to read and study, to learn exactly what God wanted for my life instead of what I wanted. I learned that the Lord would guide my life through my husband.

Almost immediately I had an opportunity to follow my husband's leading. I prayed about a car that Dusty seemed set on buying. I believed the decision he made would be from the Lord. The very next day Dusty announced that we would not be buying the car. I quietly thanked God for His answer.

I learned to keep short accounts with God. When feelings of resentment reared their ugly heads, I immediately confessed them and other wrong mental attitudes as sins, claiming Christ's promise: "If we confess our sins, He is faithful and just and will forgive us our sins and purify us from all unrighteousness" John 1:9, NIV).

Darien's knowledge of the Scriptures is exceptional. Her insight into the male ego seems phenomenal to me. Her words really hit home when she talked about accepting your husband as he is, and helping him to like himself. She said that a man who is not happy with himself cannot possibly relate correctly and lovingly toward his wife.

Right after that particular lesson I read an article in the newspaper about husbands running around on their wives. The majority of people think the reason is sex, but the report said that most straying husbands were looking for someone who would admire them, praise them, and love them as they are.

Of course, that is exactly what God commanded a wife to do. I became aware that a man needed to feel love, security, importance; then he becomes liberated to love, protect, and honor his wife. As Darien was quoting these biblical truths, I understood the need in my marriage to make Dusty feel important, admired, liberated.

Dusty was out of town for a week when I started the course. The day that he was to return, I received a call saying he wouldn't be back for two more weeks. I knew how he must have hated to call and tell me that.

Normally I would have gotten mad. This time I said

nothing unpleasant. I told him I really appreciated his calling, to take care of himself, and to get home as soon as he could. Before he hung up, I said softly, "Dusty, I love you."

At the next lesson, Darien asked us if we had ever thanked our husbands for making us a living. I certainly never had. I thought that was simply his duty.

A few nights later, Dusty called again. He began telling me how hard he had been working. This presented an excellent opportunity for me to thank him. I said, "Honey, have I ever thanked you for making us such a good living, or told you how much we appreciate the hard work you do?"

There was stunned silence on the other end. I continued the conversation, talking about the children, and asking Dusty about himself.

When he got time I began rebuilding the ego I had bruised. I told him, "You have got to have the broadest, most beautiful shoulders in the world." That was the beginning— and I am still learning. Now when there is furniture to be moved or heavy jobs to be done, I ask Dusty to do them for me. Afterward I thank him, and compliment his ability to do them so easily.

One afternoon he asked me to go to a baseball game. "I'd love to," I said. My heart almost broke as I saw his face light up. He was thrilled. I thought of the many times I had denied him my company and bound him because of it. Bound him, because there were many places he would have gone but I refused, and he didn't want to go alone.

We had a marvelous time at the game. I don't mean to imply that I fell in love with baseball. I didn't. But the joy in my husband's heart and eyes were payment enough!

Many times Dusty used to ask me to walk in the rain with him. I thought that was the dumbest idea I ever heard. Since I learned the joy of giving happiness instead of being obsessed with my own desires, he hasn't yet asked me—but you'd better believe every time it rains I sit expectantly waiting. This time, I'll go.

All during our marriage I had tried to make Dusty fill the

void in my life that I now realize only Christ can fill. By allowing Christ to enter in, all those self-centered desires that caused us so much pain and frustration have completely gone. I'm amazed how beautiful life can be when I follow God's plan for a wife. How serene life can be when a wife is under her husband's "umbrella of authority and protection," as Darien teaches.

We certainly haven't reached perfection. No one will until Christ takes us to heaven. But when we do have disagreements I have learned to say, "I'm sorry." Those two words had never been in my vocabulary where Dusty was concerned.

A few weeks ago Dusty told me he looked forward to coming home to be with me because it was so much fun. He shared how much he enjoyed our quiet times alone. *Praise the Lord*—I have waited eagerly to hear that!

I have learned the reality of appreciating my husband; I now know the magic of praise, the simple, binding beauty of the words, "thank you."

This summer we drove to Gatlinburg and took our friend Phyllis along. As we stopped for lunch, Dusty began talking. "Phyllis," he said, "you know since Chris learned God's plan for her as a woman, our marriage has completely changed. I wish next fall you would go with her to that seminar. I know you think things are over for you and Jerry, but with Christ nothing is impossible."

It is now Dusty who is recommending Darien's seminar. When we arrived in Gatlinburg, I shared with some of our friends the wonderful changes that had taken place in our relationship. I was so thrilled with what I had learned that I wanted to share these truths with other women.

I had ordered a complete set of Darien's tapes. With Dusty's encouragement I invited some friends over to begin a tape class. I was amazed at the number of women who were hungry to know God's will for their lives. We had 25 women in attendance, and this was our first attempt at a home study. Through the class, two women came to know Jesus Christ as their personal Saviour and others have written since we returned to Atlanta that they are beginning to see wonderful changes in their marriages.

I thank God for a Saviour who has completely filled the longing and void in my life. I know He can do the same for anyone who sincerely seeks Him. For those who are enmeshed in the web of self-centeredness, for those who never appreciated the man they married, for those who think that maybe they married the wrong man, I want to say . . . STOP . . . the Lord can change all that! Think for one minute what that man of yours might be if *you* became completely available to the Lord!

Well, the roar of the football crowd for my Dusty is long silent. But I thank You, Lord, that my praises will go on and on!

Reminiscing with Darien:

Chris had just returned to Atlanta after spending the summer in Gatlinburg, Tennessee, and my heart warmed as she shared how God had used her to help other women claim God's blessings for them as wives. She said, "The amazing part of it is that I didn't plan anything; it just 'happened.' That's unusual for me because I am normally a planner." I rejoiced with her over the thrills that come from being available to Christ's plan for our lives.

Chris' life parallels Eve's, the first woman, in many ways (Gen. 3). Chris never intentionally set out to hurt her husband and children. Like Eve, her downfall came from following her desires rather than God's plan. She discovered as Eve did that her actions had a far-reaching influence on her husband and children.

Our nature and desires apart from Christ's purifying power are selfish and demanding. Chris learned that Christian behavior involved more than going to church on Sunday and wanting to be a good wife and mother. She had to learn God's will through His Word, then to make His ways become a reality in her life by His power. She learned that happiness was achieved by being in right relationship with God and seeking to meet her husband's needs rather than trying to get her own needs met.

As Chris praised Dusty's admirable traits, she observed that he began to love, protect, and cherish her as never before. She helped him like himself by building his self-esteem or self-image. He, in turn, was loving her as he loved himself (Eph. 5:28–29).

Sharing Dusty's interests and hobbies made Chris a part of her husband in a deeper way. She learned the joy of sending her husband off on a weekend hunting trip because she wanted him to be happy. She now listens when he talks, not necessarily because she's enthralled with the subject but because she can discover in this way how Dusty feels and thinks.

Chris' experiences confirm that a wife regulates the home atmosphere as a thermostat controls the temperature of the house. As she seeks to comfort, encourage, and bring happiness to her family, she basks in the same benefits.

Thinking Through with You:

Question: *How does God say a good wife responds to her husband?*
Answer: "She will comfort, encourage, and do him good as long as there is life within her" (Prov. 30:12, AMP).

Q.: *What attitudes and actions of a wife build the husband's confidence?*
A.: "Let the wife see that she respects and reverences her husband—that she notices him, regards him, honors him, prefers him, venerates and esteems him; and that she defers to him, praises him, and loves and admires him exceedingly (Eph. 5:33, AMP.).

Q.: *In God's created order, what is woman's role in relation to the man?*
A.: "The woman is the glory of man" (1 Cor. 11:7, NIV).

Q.: *How will service and submission to your husband benefit both of you?*
A.: "Husbands ought to love their own wives as their own bodies. He who loves his wife loves himself. After all, no one ever hated his own body, but he feeds and cares for it" (Ephesians 5:28-29, NIV).

4

He Has the Same
Heart Toward Me

Renate Dowler

Unless you've been through it, you can't realize the turmoil of being in the middle of the ocean, leaving your homeland and family, and heading toward a strange place where your beloved awaits you.

Even now, years later, I can remember the clashing pain and happiness in my heart as I left my family in Germany and traveled toward America to join my husband-to-be.

I would lie awake nights in my stateroom, my thoughts racing faster than the propellers of the S.S. *United States* as they churned through the mighty ocean. Early in the morning I would get up and climb to the empty deck to stand quietly as the wind blew away my tears.

"Ach," I would tell myself, "how foolish you are, to feel happy and sad at the same time."

One moment my mind would be filled with thoughts of Paul, our coming marriage, and his country that would be mine. It was a wonderful place, he said.

The next moment, as I looked over the rail at the deep and ageless sea, homesickness would sweep over me.

Munich. How I loved my home. It had been so beautiful— before the war.

Until I began this long journey, every day of my life had been spent in Munich. When the air was pure and silvery, I could see the Bavarian Alps from my window.

As a child I'd perch in a windowseat and watch the people pass below—merchants rushing to deliver their wares and women pushing their baby carriages to the park.

School, skiing in the nearby mountains, church, and Christmas were memorable parts of a normal childhood in Munich. Then came Adolf Hitler and the war. Bombs fell all around us and fires burned day after horrible day, night after endless night.

When it was over, Munich was a hollow shell of her former self. One-third of her homes had been destroyed and three-quarters of her buildings were in ruins. Then the foreign occupation began.

The townspeople began to rebuild—binding up the wounds of our beautiful city. Once again the tortured earth began to spring alive with grass and trees and crops.

Our soldiers began to return, some in wooden boxes, some broken in body, and others in spirit, but like a child struggling for its first breath, we all began to live again.

Khaki uniforms, leather boots, jazz, and American faces became a constant reminder of our defeat. The G.I.s built a replacement depot near our town. It was a stop-off where soldiers were sent for reassignment to other areas or cleared for return to the States.

I began working at the depot as a clerk in the snack bar. One afternoon as I sat in the snack bar talking to my friend Helga, a tall, broad-shouldered American soldier approached our table.

"May I have a cigaret?" he asked.

We replied in German that we didn't understand. Actually, we knew what he wanted.

He pointed to the cigarets and again asked for one. I laughed and stopped my masquerade to speak to him. In broken English, I introduced Helga and myself.

He said his name was Paul, Paul Dowler.

We exchanged the usual information—where do you work, what do you do, etc. The three of us talked for awhile, and then the conversation seemed to narrow down to Paul and me. He asked me many questions about Germany, the war, customs, and personal things. He asked me to write in German things like Munich, Renate, and the main streets and theaters. We had a pleasant afternoon and then said goodbye.

One afternoon a few weeks later I saw a jeep stop in front of our house. Momma said, "Renate, that looks like an American man coming here. I wonder who he is looking for."

My heart was fluttering inside. "Momma, I know him," I said. It was Paul. I couldn't believe it.

"Well, you go out there; tell him to come on in," she ordered. She acted like inviting Americans into one's home was a normal occurrence, which it certainly wasn't.

I was terribly embarrassed. What if the neighbors should see me? At this time in Germany, a girl could ruin her reputation by dating an American. This feeling was not directed against the soldier personally; most people just felt it wasn't right to date "the enemy."

There was an old saying which still expressed the feeling in my country· "Honor that you stay in your own country and that you stay with your own people."

Neighbors' opinions, old sayings, and the like were soon forgotten, however, as I began to date the genial American on a steady basis. Paul was in the Air Police, and instead of being a temporary soldier passing through he was permanently stationed in Munich.

After the confinement of war I found almost everything fascinating outside my home. Much of our time was spent in night clubs. I had discovered dancing and I couldn't get enough. The GI bands beat out the songs popularized during those years, and we "swung and swayed" to "Now Is the Hour" and "Tuxedo Junction." For the next four years the world was ours and we savored every moment we spent together.

Then one day a piece of paper dropped like a huge oak into the gears of my merry-go-round world: Paul's new orders. Somebody in the U.S. who seemed to be related to everyone—"Uncle Sam" the boys called him—wanted Paul back in America.

Months before, Paul and I had realized that our time together was not a passing interlude. We truly and deeply loved each other. When Paul's orders came through, he asked me to return with him as his wife.

"Wife"—what a beautiful word. "Mrs. Paul Dowler"—what a beautiful sound that had.

Excitement coursed through my body as a new world flashed into view. When I returned home that afternoon my feet hardly touched the floor. I burst through the front door yelling, "Momma, Momma! Paul wants to marry me and take me home with him."

Momma faced me silently.

"Momma," I cried, "do you hear what I'm saying? Paul wants to marry me. He loves me!"

Momma sat down and waited till I calmed down. Then she said, "Renate, I want to tell you something. I think the thing you do is—you let Paul go home first, alone. You know, Paul has been away for a long time."

Momma seemed to think that perhaps Paul was just passing time with me; maybe there was a girl back in the States. Possibly he'd feel differently about me when he was again in familiar surroundings.

"Renate, you just let him go," she said, "and then wait and see if he still has the same heart toward you."

I waited as Momma asked. Then one day a letter arrived from Roswell, Georgia, U.S.A. A letter from Paul! When I opened the envelope, a bank draft for my passage fare drifted to the floor. As I read his message of love, the letter blurred before my eyes as tears of joy rolled down my cheeks.

All I could say was, "Momma, oh, Momma, Paul, he has the same heart toward me."

Now that I am older, I can understand how my family must

have dreaded seeing me off on that ship carrying me so far away. But there was no other way for me.

The long days and nights on the ship came to an end finally. I will never forget the excitement as we neared New York Harbor. The deck was crowded with passengers on their first ocean voyage, and they were filled with the awe and expectation of a child at his first Christmas.

There she stood, the Statue of Liberty, the symbol of everything this land of promise held for us. There were tears and cries of joy, each person reacting in his own way. What a day!

"Oh, America," I thought, "you are truly beautiful."

In New York City I boarded a train to Atlanta, Georgia, where Paul awaited me. I met Paul's family—his mother Ruth, his brother Donald, and his sister Carol. They were all so warm and welcoming.

Ruth helped me so much with our wedding plans. She contacted the minister of her church, who arranged to perform our ceremony in his study.

The big day came. As I got ready, standing before the mirror, I wished that Momma and my sisters could be with me to share my wedding day. My dress was white linen with long, graceful sleeves. I'd put my long, dark hair up in a large bun and fluffed out curls all around my face.

During the service I looked every minute at Paul. He looked so handsome with his sparkling blue eyes and dark-blond hair. So neat and distinguished in his blue serge suit.

After the ceremony we said our good-byes to Paul's family and enjoyed a quiet dinner before driving to the Henry Grady Hotel where we spent our wedding night.

The splendor of that day was going to have to last a long time, for we rented a small, old apartment in the Buckhead area of Atlanta. Three dull-gray rooms with hardwood floors and bare walls became our first home.

Paul carried a complete course in law school and then worked a full-time job in the afternoons and evenings. There was just enough money to fill our basic needs. But it was thrilling as we began our life together—and such fun.

A friend of Ruth's donated an iron bed. And an old dresser was rescued from somebody's garage. At first there was no table to eat at nor chairs to sit on. We were the proud owners of two spoons and two knives; most of our meals were eaten from cans as we dined on our big iron bed!

One day I had the opportunity to do some sewing for a lady who lived near us. I took great pains to make every stitch perfect. When finished I received four dollars for my work!

What a grand time I had with that money! I bought a 75-cent aluminum coffee pot, a hammer, two dishes, and a cannister set.

I'm sure the emperors of Rome, lying on satin pillows and feasting on grapes, could not have known the pleasure that Paul and I shared during those days.

I suppose we could have used extra money, but I never went to work. Paul never wanted me to take a job, and I considered it a real privilege to stay home. My experience as a child contributed to my attitude about working wives. My mother worked in a mill during my childhood and I silently resented it. Daddy was a hard-working man who provided well for his family. Momma worked because of her desire for unnecessary extras.

I was jealous of my friends whose mothers stayed home. Their mothers were always there to pack their lunch and slip in that special piece of cake baked early in the morning, and at home to greet them when school was out.

There was always work for me with Momma gone so much —dishes, cooking, and cleaning. And those important talks— moments to share a special joy or disappointment—didn't fit well into Momma's schedule. I determined then that if I ever married, even if we had to eat beans out of a can, I'd never work outside my home.

Between Paul's work and his studies, we had very little time together. Aching loneliness took root in my soul. I felt, "Here I am in America in a three-room apartment with nothing to do." Some days I'd wax and rewax the floors just to keep busy. And the ache grew.

Some afternoons I'd stand by the window watching cars returning home from the day's work. I would think back to Germany and wish, "Oh, if I could just go home." It was a confused feeling I couldn't understand because I was happy with Paul; we had a beautiful marriage.

My desolate feeling was soon replaced by a wonderful one: I discovered I was expecting a baby.

Paul and I were blessed with a beautiful, blue-eyed, black-haired girl. We named her Anna. That baby was the biggest thrill of my life.

Paul was so busy that I immersed myself with the baby. I would read to her and we would play. My life revolved around Anna. For a time she quenched all my feelings of loneliness.

One evening after I'd put Anna to bed, I walked through the living room and was attracted by music coming from the TV. Like many other "poor" people, we had a big TV.

On the television screen I saw a stately looking man standing before a massive crowd and singing the most beautiful song I'd ever heard. The words, "Blessed assurance, Jesus is mine," floated through the room.

When the singer concluded, another tall, dignified man appeared and began speaking. It was Billy Graham.

I didn't know Billy Graham then. I'd never heard of him, and I didn't realize he was a minister. If I had known who he was, I wouldn't have listened because I had "my religion" and I wasn't looking for anything else.

The program was coming from a place called Madison Square Garden. Beyond the speaker's stand was a huge poster that read, "I Am the Way, the Truth, and the Life." Like the words Mr. Graham was speaking, I understood the meaning, but they had no relevance for me.

The only reason I watched was my hope of hearing more of that beautiful song. When the program ended, the announcer said they would be on again the following week.

I faithfully tuned in for the next couple of weeks, waiting for that song from George Beverly Shea. The song wasn't sung, but one evening as I watched, everything changed.

Mr. Graham was talking about the feeling of loneliness that I had experienced. He would say "lonely," and I completely identified with what he said. I still didn't know he was a minister. He could have said "The Bible says . . ." all evening long and it wouldn't have meant anything to me. We had many prayer books in our home, but no Bible. No one had ever taught us from the Bible, and I had never held one in my hand. I didn't even realize what it was—God's Word.

As he spoke I thought, "He's smart. I would really like to talk to him." There were feelings in me that I couldn't identify till he named them. The mysterious ache in my heart had proved that all the nice things in my life couldn't make me happy.

On previous telecasts I'd watched people go forward at the end of Mr. Graham's talk, and I wondered what they were doing. This time I thought, "If I were there, I would follow those people so I could talk to that man."

At that point Billy turned from the crowd and looked at me from the television screen. "You, there in the living room . . ." he said. That's where I was—and I felt he was talking to me personally. "You, too," he said, "if you have never accepted Jesus Christ as your Saviour you can do that right now!"

Paul was still at work and Anna was asleep. Slowly I slipped to my knees by the sofa and began to pray. I don't remember what I said; I wanted whatever that man had, whatever he was talking about.

I wept and I prayed. Sometime later I got up and turned the television off. I didn't want to be disturbed; I had such a beautiful, peaceful feeling. I just wanted to bathe myself in it.

The next week after watching Mr. Graham, I wrote down the address given by the announcer. I wanted to send this wonderful man a gift so I sent a whole dollar! I thought that was a lot.

His Minneapolis office began to send me little booklets called "Decision." I devoured each one as it came. At the back of each was a space to write your name and address if you'd made a decision for Christ. Each time I filled out all the blanks and then tucked the booklet away for safe keeping.

One evening a few weeks later I was sitting on the front porch when a car drove slowly by, stopped, and backed up. A young man got out and walked toward me. "There is a lady who looks like she needs a Bible," he announced. He said he had just finished work and was on his way home when he saw me.

I had never thought about a Bible, but I said, "Well, I need a Bible."

"What type of Bible do you want?" he asked. He said he had a King James Bible and a Catholic Bible.

I thought for a moment and said, "I think I'll take one of those King James kind." It was a huge, family-size Bible, but it felt light in my hands.

That evening I couldn't wait to read this book of God. I put Anna to bed and went to the kitchen with my big book. Opening it on our oilcloth-covered table, I began reading in "Revelation." I struggled through the whole book, noting seven-this and seven-that. "My goodness!" I thought, "I wonder what this is all pointing to," but continued on undiscouraged.

Soon after I had an intense desire to take Anna to church. Because of my religious background, I felt infants must be in church. I shared my feelings with Paul. As he and I were from very different backgrounds, we decided not to attend either of our former churches. We began to visit various churches that were new to us.

One had a minister who wore a robe and I felt at home. Having been raised in a ritualistic church, I found it almost impossible to listen to a minister if he wasn't wearing one. Yet I wasn't interested in listening to a preacher the night

I first tuned in to Billy Graham. I'm sure that if he had been wearing a robe he would never have caught me!

In time Paul and I moved into our first real home, and the Lord provided a Christian friend in my new neighborhood. Jan had a strong influence in my life. When I did not understand a verse in Scripture, she would patiently explain each word.

I was still reading from my giant Bible. I just drank it in. Some nights I propped myself up on my elbows in bed and read until 2 or 3 A.M. One evening Paul said, "Momma, you're going to need a smaller Bible." The very next day he bought me a small white one at the dime store. I was so proud of it.

Realizing what Bible study meant to me, I approached Jan with a new idea. "Stanley parties, Tupperware parties," I said, "why can't we have a party for the Lord? Let's get together and all of us will bring our Bibles and we'll sing and read the Bible together."

It turned out to be one of the sweetest times of fellowship, and I grew in my knowledge of God's Word. Those "parties for the Lord" continued for three years.

Our next-door neighbor, Ginny, attended our Bible study, and one evening after a visit I offered to walk home with her because her husband was away. She appreciated my company while she checked out her lonely house.

As we entered the hall, she said, "Renate, don't go until I get my gun out." Her husband had given her a revolver to make her feel safer. Reaching for the gun, her hand knocked it off the closet shelf and it hit the floor with an explosive crack! Pain ripped through my stomach and I sank to the floor. I grasped at the wound as blood flowed, and Ginny screamed, "Oh, my God, no!" She ran out of the house to get Paul. Soon the door flew open and Paul rushed in, pale but in control. He carried me to the car and raced for Piedmont Hospital.

As the car wheels whined over the pavement, Psalm 23 ran through my mind over and over almost as if the Lord had turned on a record for my heart. I knew I could die, but I had the sweetest peace; there was no fear at all.

I realized at this moment that Christ was the most important person in my life. Through the past three years this relationship had become more and more important, but I am strong-willed and I still had areas of my life in which I felt quite self-sufficient. Now, recognizing my desperate dependence on the Lord, my will was broken and I acknowledged that "all things do work together for good."

The doctors were frank with Paul. "She has a fifty-fifty chance. We just want you to be prepared."

Many prayers went up in my behalf during the crisis, and the Lord spared me.

When I was well enough to go out again, a friend took me to a neighborhood Bible class meeting in her area of Atlanta. The teacher was Darien Cooper. I wasn't at all sure I liked her authoritative approach. But she taught God's Word with a depth and conviction that I'd never heard. Her personal knowledge of Christ was reflected in everything she said.

I returned week after week, finding freedom from many ignorant hang-ups I'd acquired. She taught Ephesians in a thrilling way, and I first understood the Spirit-filled life as she taught from Romans. She opened so many doors of understanding that I have continued through the years to bring other women to her classes. I knew nothing about God's role for a wife until I heard Darien teaching it.

Paul was a Christian and always gentle with me. Because he disliked arguments, I usually got my way. In our earlier years I made the decisions on where we went and what we did. If Paul's suggestions didn't suit me, I'd persist until we agreed on my choice.

Our biggest area of disagreement was always Anna. When she was disobedient and needed a whipping, I'd beg, "Please, Paul, don't whip her, please."

"But she needs to be spanked," he'd say.

"No, you might hurt her."

"Renate, don't you know I wouldn't actually hurt her?"

I thought he'd spank her so hard he'd knock her kidneys loose or something—silly, real to me. I'd object until Paul gave up. Time after time it happened, and I thought I was protecting Anna.

Since I'd assumed the position of authority, Anna came to me when she got out of line and asked me to talk to her daddy. She knew that if she got her way with me I would handle Paul.

The few times I allowed Paul to spank Anna, she'd scream and scream so I'd feel her suffering. I'd go out in the backyard and stick my fingers in my ears; I just couldn't stand her crying.

When our arguments over Anna's disobedience got hot, Paul would say, "You'll be sorry one of these days," and walk out. He would sit in the yard, go to the basement, or just disapppear for ten or fifteen minutes. In time he'd return and say, "How about a cup of coffee, Momma?" I'd say, "OK." This coffee offering became our peace-making ritual. We never discussed our problems—we just poured coffee on them!

When Anna was 13, she began to develop a rebellious spirit. Boys, parties, and popularity became the prime interests in her life. One evening she supposedly left for a party at a girlfriend's house. About ten o'clock the phone rang and Paul answered. The blood drained from his face as he hung up the receiver.

"Who was it?" I asked.

"The police," he said in a quavering voice.

"What's happened?'

"I'll tell you on the way. Get your coat," he said. But a cold silence filled the car as we drove downtown.

Speaking to the police officer in charge, we found that Anna had been to a party, but her friend's parents weren't home. Drinking had begun early, and as the night progressed the house was completely torn apart. Neighbors had called the police because of the loud music. There was two thousand dollars worth of damage done to the house—but our concern was that Anna was safe.

Tears trickled down Anna's cheeks as we drove her home. The ordeal had been so frightening that I felt she had suffered enough.

I recognized that Anna had serious problems, and my solution was to nag at her. I'd demand changes and threaten punishment but never follow through. Like my mother before me, I was all talk and no action. Anna knew this and continued her rebellious ways.

It was a few years later that I heard from Darien about God's plan for me as a wife and mother. My heart broke as I realized how wrong my interference in Anna's discipline had been. Under Darien's teachings I began to adopt the principles set forth in God's Word. I stored each and every truth, not imagining how much I'd need them.

The situation with Anna continued to deteriorate. She cut classes at school and her honor roll grades dropped until she was hardly passing. She no longer looked lovely and feminine. Taking a bath became a traumatic experience for her.

There were symptoms all along the way, but I didn't know the danger signals. When Paul tried to intervene, I'd assure him: "She's in a different generation;" or, "She's only trying to impresss her friends." I really believed it.

Anna's slender figure all of a sudden began to fill out with unbecoming fat. She became moody, cheerful one day and down the next. She'd eat everything in the house and then not eat for days. Or lie in bed sleeping her life away, then spend periods of sleepless nights. I didn't know then that marijuana was making her very hungry, accounting for her weight gain, nor that she had begun to take amphetamines, accounting for her sleepless nights.

At 17, Anna had been dating a boy that Paul and I very much disapproved of. He was from a "good family" and attended one of Atlanta's outstanding private schools, but his affluent background was not apparent in his sloppy dress, rude manners, and lack of respect for his parents. He and

Anna left one evening for a movie. I wasn't to see her again for four days!

She was supposed to be home at midnight. When the clock struck one, fear began to swell inside me. The minutes and hours crept by . . . two . . . three . . . four o'clock . . . and an icy chill ran through me as the ringing of the phone broke into my quandary.

It was Anna. "Momma, let me talk to Daddy," she cried.

I called Paul to the phone and I listened to the conversation on the bedroom extension. She had been charged with possession of marijuana and accessory to car theft, she said. It seemed like hours passed as Anna begged for assistance and Paul talked.

I heard him say, "Anna, this is the very thing we tried to keep you from. This is why your Momma and I have counseled so with you. You didn't want to listen. You wanted your own way. You said you were going to do your own thing. Well, darling, you have arrived at the end of the road we tried to keep you from traveling. I'm sorry, but you'll just have to stay there . . . or call some of those friends you've been hanging around with. Baby, I'm sorry. We love you, but we won't bail you out of this one."

Thoughts and Bible principles kept flying through my mind. "Obey your husband, obey your husband," God said. "Don't let emotions run your life," echoed from my lessons with Darien Cooper.

When Paul hung up he slumped into a chair with a heavy sadness. My own heart was breaking for my child. Frightening thoughts and pictures whirled through my thoughts. I had heard about horrid jail conditions. I envisioned Anna coming in contact with hardened criminals or perverts.

I prayed: "Father, in James 1:5 You say 'If any of you lacks wisdom, he should ask God . . . and it will be given to him.' Dear Father, I claim that promise for Paul and me right now. Give us the wisdom to handle this situation for Your glory and Anna's benefit. I ask that you make me willing to accept this decision Paul has made. Father, I'm trusting Anna to You. You protect her. You draw her to Yourself. In Christ's name, Amen."

As each new day came, Anna would call for help, and each time Daddy would say, "No."

During this time the Lord so beautifully kept His Word and His promises before us. Our home was calm, with a "peace that passes understanding."

Four days leter as Paul and Anna talked, I heard him say, "I'll see what I can do."

When he hung up, he said simply, "She's broken."

A few hours later, a tired but calm girl reentered our home. I took Anna in my arms and we both wept with blessed relief.

"Momma," she said, "you know when Daddy refused to come get me, I got so scared. There was a pain of loneliness shooting through my whole body. But, Momma, last night something happened. I realized the mess I was in; I knew I had gotten here all on my own. I thought back to the talks you and Daddy had with me. How you'd told me about Jesus and His love. I thought that by becoming a Christian I'd lose all my freedom, all my individuality. Sitting in that jail cell, I knew that grass had been warping my view. Amphetamines were twisting my decisions. Pressure from my friends motivated my actions. And sitting behind bars was far from being free. I hadn't been in control at all—I saw it. You know what I did, Momma?"

"No; what did you do, Baby?"

"I got down on my knees before God and all the women in my cell and prayed. I said, 'Lord, it's just You and me now. You're the only One who can help me. Momma and Daddy told me about You, so right now, Lord Jesus, I'm trusting You for me.' After that, a real peace settled. I'm so sorry I've hurt you and Daddy, but with Jesus I know things will be different."

It was time for my confession. "Anna," I said, "I want to apologize to you, too. I so wanted you to be happy that I often interfered with your daddy's discipline. I'm sure you could have learned this lesson much younger and in a much less devastating way if I hadn't been so out of line."

We stood there, silently facing each other and holding hands. There were no more words, but an inner "Thank You, Lord." At that moment the Lord broke through our generation gap.

Each day Christ molds and shapes Anna into the beautiful woman He is creating. His presence has touched every part of her life. The rebellious will is broken. Through an undrugged mind, she is again making good grades.

The old group is gone. Anna learned the truth of Proverbs 13:20: "He who walks [as a companion] with wise men shall be wise, but he who associates with [self-confident] fools will [be a fool himself and] shall smart for it" (AMP).

Before I learned my position as a Christian wife, before I understood Christ's chain of authority, I would have reacted much differently to a crisis with Anna—possibly sentencing our precious daughter to disaster. Christ has been so patient with each of us.

Each time Darien begins a new session of her course, Paul joins me in inviting women to attend. My car is always loaded with a new group, and secretly I anticipate how beautiful those faces will be when they see what Christ has waiting for them.

I know there will be times when I stumble, but I know, too, that Christ will always have "the same heart" of love toward me.

Reminiscing with Darien:

God was gracious in giving me such a precious friend as Renate. Initially I was captivated by her radiant love for Jesus Christ and her unreserved care for others. She literally glows with excitement for the Christian life; boredom isn't in her vocabulary. At almost every Bible class she joyfully shared a fresh truth or insight she'd gained from God's Word. Her simple, straight-forward way of presenting these truths could cut deep into one's heart and at the same time stir praise to God.

Even as a new Christian, Renate seemed to sense that the way to grow spiritually was to know and trust God's Word, not others' experiences. An emotion or experience can change with one's physical health, emotional state, or spiritual condition. "Good" experiences can even be counterfeited by Satan! Spiritual guidelines should never be based on them. God has provided knowledge of His will through passages, principles, and doctrines in His Word. The Holy Spirit enables the receptive spirit to understand and apply these truths in daily life.

For real stability in life, it is essential that God's way of thinking becomes ours. This is accomplished by transferring God's truths from His printed Word to our minds. Without this personal knowledge of God's Word, our thoughts and actions will be conformed to this world's flawed ways. (Romans 12:1, 2)

Renate had interfered with God's most gentle form of leading a child: the father's authority in the home. Therefore God used a harsher authority, civil law, to break Anna's rebellious will. When one learns to submit to human authority, it is much easier to be obedient to Christ's authority in our spiritual life. Anna missed this privilege in her early years.

Through her mother's new obedience to Paul, Anna is helped to be obedient to her parents. Renate realizes that Anna's attitude toward authority is more important than the particular issue being discussed. Isn't it sobering to realize that children learn important attitudes from their parents!

Should you meet Renate, you'll recognize her by her love for God's Word. She's walking evidence that "man shall not live by bread alone, but on every word that proceeds out of the mouth of God" (Matt. 4:4).

Thinking Through with You:

Question: *What is a big clue—to you and God—as to the real person you are?*
Answer: "As he thinks within himself, so he is" (Proverbs 23:7, NASB).

Q.: *How explicitly has God provided so that His thoughts and ways may become ours?*
A.: "All Scripture is inspired by God and profitable for teaching, for reproof, for correction, for training in righteousness; that the man of God may be adequate, equipped for every good work" (2 Tim. 3:16-17, NASB).

Q.: *Why should you study God's Word?*
A.: "Your Word have I laid up in my heart, that I might not sin against You" (Ps. 119:11, AMP.).

Q.: *How may we gain a greater appetite for the spiritual food of God's Word?*
A.: "Taste and see that the Lord is good; blessed is the man who trusts in Him" (Ps. 34:8 BERK).

5

View Through
A Bottle

Duanne Freig

The waves were draped in hues of gold, orange, and pink as the sun dipped below the horizon. Jon and I had spent many evenings like this, holding hands, walking the beach, talking, and planning. Through the past year of dating we had become soul-mates in the purest sense of the word. But this day was different.

The beach was the same, the waves still beat rhythmically against the shore, but anguish brimmed in our hearts. Jon was going away to Duke University, and it seemed so far from Miami. He'd become such a part of my life that the idea of being separated was almost more than I could bear. We left the beach that day knowing that months would separate our next moments together.

With Jon in North Carolina, my senior year in high school crept by. Our letters challenged the capacity of the U.S. Postal Service. Even at long distance, we decided we wanted a spring wedding. Jon's parents, however, felt Jon should complete his education before marriage, and we reluctantly agreed to wait.

For graduation, my parents gave me a trip to North Carolina. I would stay with Jon's sister, who lived near the university. As the bus whizzed over the flat openness of north Florida, past the tall buildings in Atlanta, and into the rolling hills of North Carolina, my thoughts were constantly on Jon.

We had a beautiful reunion—there was so much to talk about, so many things to share, and so much love to express! As we discussed our loneliness, the promises we'd made to delay marriage began to evaporate.

Jon suddenly ruffled my hair and said, "Sweetheart, let's stop all this talking and get married!"

"Married?" I said.

"Yes, some of the guys told me about a justice of the peace not far from here. There's no reason to wait; I love you and I want you for my wife. There is no point in upsetting our parents, so we'll just keep it our secret."

"Oh, Jon, yes, yes," I exclaimed.

This day was to be a mixture of joy and regret. In front of a business-like justice of the peace, Jon and I became husband and wife. I was full of love for him, but my heart ached for the beautiful wedding I had dreamed of, which now I would never have.

A few weeks after I returned home, I found that rising each morning was a chore. Waves of nausea greeted me each new day. I didn't need a doctor to tell me that I was carrying Jon's child. As soon as I shared the news with Jon, he returned to Miami.

A few days later, I stood in front of my parents' house waving goodbye to Jon as he drove off in his blue sports car for Montgomery, Alabama, to tell his parents about our marriage.

Jon's parents, Bill and Edith, had made a new life for themselves in this country. They had left Belgium when Hitler's armies invaded. His father had established a thriving restaurant business, and his mother devoted herself to the family.

Jon's father wasn't home when he arrived. Jon told his mother about our marriage, and she took the news well, but she convinced Jon it would be better if she told Bill. Jon's father drank heavily and had high blood pressure, and she wasn't sure how he would react. She was afraid, and her fear kept her from breaking the news. Jon finally told his dad in a letter—not the best way to start out with one's in-laws!

Jon left Duke and took a job in Miami with a large engineering firm. We found a darling apartment near Haulover Beach, and for the next two years we lived contentedly. Our baby's birth completed the circle of our happiness.

The first time we visited Jon's parents after our marriage, Bill welcomed me with genuine warmth. Unfortunately, there was a strain between Edith and me from the beginning.

Our ethnic backgrounds made a great difference in our ideas and opinions. I found that one doesn't marry just a man; one truly marries into a family, for better or for worse!

Yet my disagreements with Edith seemed minor compared with the arguments Jon had with his father on subsequent visits.

Bill felt that we should move to Montgomery. He wanted to pass his restaurant business on to his son, and he expected Jon to respect his wishes. Jon didn't want to change jobs, and Bill was determined to make him. After a few drinks and Jon's continued refusal, Bill would storm: "How come you don't care about me? If you had any decency you'd take over the place I've prepared for you!"

One day Jon received a call from Bill. He wanted us to move to Montgomery so Jon could work in the newest restaurant he wanted to buy. Bill said he needed Jon to help carry the work load.

After discussing it, we decided to give it a try. But we decided that Jon would take a regular job and help Bill in his spare time until we knew if "restauranting" was what we really wanted.

I was enthralled by the beauty of southern Alabama. The tall oaks and cedars draped in Spanish moss made me feel a part of the graceful past.

We had hardly unpacked our suitcases when Jon informed me he wouldn't seek other employment. His father had persuaded him to go directly into the restaurant business full-time.

Our original understanding was shattered and I was deeply hurt. I felt Jon had betrayed my trust and I very much resented the influence of his father. I felt Jon had no right to make this decision without consulting me.

Almost overnight, the strained relationship between Jon and Bill changed. They found a new friendship through socializing. Drinking and staying out late seemed to be a part of every business deal!

My fascination with the spreading oaks, Spanish moss, and graceful mansions wore off. This beautiful country had become a threat. I complained to Jon, telling him that I wanted to go home. Our arguments became frequent. I'd tell Jon I was sorry we'd ever moved, that since our move our marriage was going down the drain.

Material gains weren't worth what was happening to us, I tried to explain. I was lonely, I felt isolated in the unfamiliar surroundings, and I didn't like him to be away from home night after night.

When Jon was drinking—which seemed to be most of the time—he'd blame me. "You're never satisfied! You're always complaining," he'd shout. When sober, he would see things as they were and tell me, "I know I treat you bad, but things are going to be different." But they weren't, and I saw Jon starting down the same road his father had gone. I felt miserable and trapped, and my anguished complaints just seemed to drive Jon out more and more.

I shared my fears with the only person I was close to, Jon's mother. She had compensated for lonely hours and lack of love through her daughter and grandchildren. I knew that could never provide a substitute for me.

Jon and Bill would get together with business friends for lunch, have a few drinks, and add a few more until the afternoon was gone. They'd move from the Diplomat to the Embers and on and on. It was a time of high living for Jon.

Many midnights passed while I waited up for Jon, and

usually he would come in drunk. I had never known anyone
with an alcohol problem and I was incapable of coping with
it. Our late-night arguments followed a pattern:

"Where have you been? Why didn't you call?"

"I've been out getting drunk and I'm stoned."

"Jon, I want a divorce. I simply can't live this way."

"Get one. I don't care. Get one; just walk out and leave."

It wasn't any use fighting. Nothing ever changed. He
wouldn't leave and I felt that I couldn't leave because of the
children. I know he wanted me to stay but to allow him
to behave as he pleased.

Many times I felt like calling Mom and Dad and asking
them if I could come home. Then I'd realize they had no idea
we were having problems. As far as they knew, we were
blissfully happy, and deep down I hated for them to think
badly of Jon. It was hell on earth for me; I didn't know whom
to turn to or what to do.

I needed Jon so much, his love, his attention, the talks we
used to have. As his drinking increased, our sex life almost
came to a halt. When Jon did make attempts at physical love,
half of me would be thrilled but the other half would be so
bitter that I couldn't respond to him.

One evening we attended a glittering party given by one
of Jon's business associates. It was held in a back yard, and
Chinese lanterns swung gracefully from huge oaks. The reflections danced on the ripples of a pool. It was the same old
crowd with the same old problems, but something was
different.

Jon had wandered off, talking, drink in hand, leaving me
sitting alone. I watched the people like actors in a play, and
felt absolutely isolated. The lilting voice of Dionne Warwick
whispered the words of "A House is Not a Home," and the
message cut deep.

"Doanne," a voice said. I looked up and saw a tall, quite
attractive man, some years my senior. We'd met briefly once
before. It was common knowledge that he had long-standing
marital problems.

He said, "You are looking even more attractive than the last time I saw you." My nerves leaped. I was hungry for masculine compliments and attention; it had been so long since Jon had given me any. I thanked him for the compliment, and he called me "adorable" and invited me to lunch. We sat and talked for a long time. The conversation was liberally seasoned with flattering, flirting overtones. The evening was going to my head.

I never gave him a clear answer on the lunch offer. I think I wanted to go—but I was afraid. Only my inbred morality stopped me. The right part of me thought "No," but the wrong part of me was saying, "Why not? What else is left for you? You're young. You're attractive. What are you going to do—wait all your life for Jon?"

Before my wrong side could win, I discovered I was expecting our third child. I considered this the worst thing that could happen. Our youngest was just 18 months old, and the thought of having two babies devastated me. When I shared the news with Jon, he was jolted too. But he never knew how the pregnancy shattered my morale. I had just gotten my weight down and was feeling I looked attractive when the bad news shredded my struggling pride.

Jon's drinking and staying out became worse. The pregnancy plus our problems continually drained me. I'd stay up until three or four o'clock in the morning waiting for Jon, dying inside night by night. The mental torment was almost more than I could bear.

When our daughter was born, she was ill and the doctors feared she had spinal meningitis and wouldn't live. At this point I made a weak attempt at prayer, but I didn't know God. It was one of those, "God, help me; I've got in over my head" prayers. It turned out that the baby wasn't as seriously ill as the doctors thought.

I felt guilty because I hadn't wanted the baby, but in my need seeds were planted in my heart which would take root later. My doctor tried to calm me during the crisis with the baby, but instead of tranquilizers he prescribed: "Try prayer,

Doanne; God can do much more for you than drugs ever can." I was impressed because I respected Dr. Lawrence, and I'd never heard a doctor talk like that. I thought long about this, and the words became implanted in the inner reaches of my mind.

After our daughter's recovery, things began to fall into the same old disorder. But God had begun to draw me to Himself.

Six weeks later, my sister's illness was to make me realize how temporal this life is. It was a comparatively quiet Sunday afternoon when the telephone rang. Jon answered and when he hung up he told me that my sister was in the hospital. She had cancer and they had already removed her right breast.

I screamed, "O God, no," and collapsed in tears. Everything inside of me cried out for God's help. I knew there had to be more. For the first time in my life, my eyes turned from my wretched situation to God alone, and the best I knew how, I asked Him into my life.

I began to going to a nearby church. I had been born into a family that taught the moral "rights and wrongs," but there was no earnest discussion or personal knowledge of Jesus Christ. Hungrily I began to read my Bible, to seek God's will, and to pray.

One woman who attended this church, Linda, obviously knew Jesus Christ personally. She stood out in the crowd of once-a-week church attenders. I sought her out and shared with her the fact that I'd just turned my life over to God and I wanted to grow.

Linda introduced me to her friend Sara who was also a Christian. Through these friends, I found growth, instruction, and a new church where God's Word was taught faithfully.

I first noticed a change in myself one day when I spilled boiling water on my foot. The old Doanne would have cussed a blue streak. But I just thought, "Gee, does that hurt!" I found myself hurrying through my housework so that I could read my Bible and spend a quiet time with God.

One afternoon I was reading in Matthew and pondering

the meaning of chapter 10, verse 36. It said, "And a man's foes shall be they of his own household." I puzzled at this because I felt close to my family and couldn't understand how they could ever be against me for becoming a Christian. I was soon to learn its meaning.

In my new role as a Christian, I had begun caring for my husband's needs rather than nurturing my own disappointments. Jon questioned me about the change in attitude. "Doanne, you look different," he said, "what's happened to you?"

I felt that now was the time to tell him. "Jon, I've found Christ. I've repented of my sins. I'm not afraid of death. There's something more, Jon!"

He got terribly angry. I could see it swelling up in his eyes. Sullenly he answered, "We're different. We're growing apart."

I wondered how much further apart we could possibly get, but still his words hurt. I then recalled what I had read in Matthew that morning and I knew God had been preparing me for Jon's reaction. As I focused my thoughts and faith in Christ, I was flooded with the peace and assurance that He had our marriage well in hand.

From that evening on Jon got worse. His drinking increased. Before, he'd come home drunk and I would do the hollering; now he'd yell and curse me.

The more the battle raged in Jon, the more peace the Lord seemed to give me. During this time I could take anything he could dish out and still be happy because for the first time my happiness wasn't dependent on Jon's actions and moods. But my faith was tested more severely as I heard Jon say things and watched him do things I never dreamed would come from him.

Jon came in one morning, dead drunk, with flames of hostility blazing in his heart. Using the phone downstairs, he asked the operator to ring our number. When I answered on the bedroom phone, he said, "Listen you———, come down here and make my dinner." I thought, "Lord, help me do this." It was 4 A.M. and I had to grit my teeth to remain composed, but I went down and fixed his dinner.

My calm attitude angered him more. He was feeling guilty and he wanted me to lash back and justify his own rotten actions.

He tried to provoke me with crude conversation, but I was rejoicing inside because I could see the conviction of the Lord showering down on him. I knew that as long as I could behave in obedience to the Lord, *He* would deal with Jon. I prayed, "Lord, help me learn this lesson now. I don't want to wander in the wilderness for 40 years like the Israelites did." It was hard at times to respond lovingly to Jon's outbursts, but each time that I held my tongue the next time was easier. It is difficult to describe what Christ did during this time except to say He provided a "peace that passes all understanding."

It was truly a troubled, puzzling time. One moment Jon would curse me and in the next he would say, "You're really wonderful and I'm glad for the peace you've found. Maybe someday it will happen to me—just not right now. I'm not ready." Tears would well up in his eyes and there would be aching silence.

Over a period of ten months, the conflict inside Jon raged on. There were times when my immature knowledge of Christianity put more strain on our relationship. Soon after coming to know Christ, I began to change overt things that I felt weren't the "Christian" thing to do. I lost my desire to go to cocktail parties, so I refused to accompany Jon to them. Jon reacted strongly to this "holier-than-thou" attitude. Without words, I was telling him, "What you are doing is wrong. I don't approve of you or your actions." He couldn't comprehend what was happening to me, and I spoiled my mute testimony by giving him the idea that Christianity was a collection of no-no's.

I was so hungry for God's Word that I read my Bible often. In the evening when I went to bed I read. The picture of me sitting in bed reading my Bible stirred more anger and recrimination in Jon. He struck out verbally because I was making the difference between us more pronounced. I had decided to do what I thought was Christian whether Jon liked it or not.

At a series of neighborhood Bible studies I began to realize that my dogmatic approach was wrong. Friends lent me helpful books, and I listened to teaching tapes. I learned it was my place to submit to my husband. I found that I didn't know anything about the role of a Christian wife.

Christ honored my struggling attempts and immature faith by continual encouragement. He gave me the willingness and love to obey my husband in whatever he asked. It seemed that the Lord cut down the flow of party invitations, but when we did go the Lord provided opportunities for me to share my faith. While Jon was socializing, the Lord often brought someone my way who was hungry to find the same answers I had found.

As the Lord slowly changed my attitudes and responses and gave me a deeper love for my husband, Jon revolted more and more. He knew how to interact with the old Doanne, but the new Doanne upset all his calculations. He retaliated with fiendish ingenuity, and his tactics would have conquered me if Christ had not been recasting my life. Because of Him, there was love instead of manipulation, stability instead of fragility. But I didn't have complete victory yet.

One morning Jon left for work and I didn't see him until the next evening. He had left the office with his friend, Joe; they had gotten drunk and hopped a plane to California. He bought a round-trip ticket for both of them. This foolishness came to well over $600.

As the hours crept by that night, Joe's wife began calling, terribly upset, looking for him. I was praying, trying to keep my thoughts on the Lord and asking Him to keep my husband safe wherever he was. Jon later told me that they began to sober up during the flight and decided they'd better go home. So they had spent all that money and hadn't even got off the plane!

When they returned to Montgomery, Jon got drunk again before returning home. He had Joe call me to come to the airport and pick them up. Weary of trusting Christ to handle our problems, I exploded: "I don't care if you two hop the next plane out!" and I hung up.

I guess I was thinking, "Well, Lord, I appreciate all You've done up to this point, but at the moment I've had it, and thank You very much, but I'll handle this one." I felt that such a financial loss was too much to bear.

The tension and pressure of the night's events overwhelmed me and my old self-pity returned. I told my friends, Jon's parents, the neighbors, the preacher, and anyone who would listen what Jon had done to me. They consoled me with comments like, "You poor girl, you have really gone through it." I knew I was fast slipping away from the spiritual walk I'd known, but I couldn't and wouldn't give up this martyred feeling. I got such gratification from the self-pity that I continued to slide.

Hoping to help, my friend Sue invited me to church for prayer. I recall telling her on the way that God ought to give me a good chastening because I had allowed myself to sink into such indulgence and despair.

When we arrived at the church, people were quietly praying in various pews. I sat down in one of the pews, bowed my head and closed my eyes . . . but that was it. I felt spiritually blank. I thought, "I am wasting my time sitting here. My prayers aren't getting through." I just felt terribly apathetic.

Then during the worship service, a missionary sitting beside me turned, looked me directly in the face and began speaking. "God is all you need, but you are drinking from other fountains and your capacity to receive from God is very small." I had never seen him before, nor have I seen him since, but I knew that God was directing this to me and my needs. In that moment I turned from the frustrations and self-pity I had been indulging in and claimed God's forgiveness. My rebellion drained out as if someone had pulled a plug.

When I got home I picked up my Bible and opened it to Hebrews 12:6, which says, "For the Lord corrects and disciplines everyone whom He loves, and He punishes, even scourges, every son whom He accepts and welcomes to His heart and cherishes" (AMP). I felt that verse was for me personally. I cried and cried and thanked God for bringing me back. I began to prepare myself and my home for Jon's return from work.

The California escapade, which had seemed to be such a curse, was the beginning of a turning point for us. Later when Jon and I talked he said that it had shocked him into some sense of reality. He said that for the first time he realized he wasn't controlling the drinking!

Up-down-up, the roller coaster went on. But now during Jon's sober periods we would have long, quiet talks as we did in our earlier years. Yet coming off the bottle was desperately hard, and in a matter of days he was failing again.

At a family get-together, Jon was criticized by his parents for neglecting his family and his job. During the argument that followed, Jon jumped up and shouted that he wanted all of us to get off his back.

He slammed the door behind him and set out walking the 12 miles home. I got in the car and drove alongside, begging him to let me drive him home. Through sobs he said, "Just go away. I want to be left alone." I tried to reason with him. "Jon, please get in the car. Let's talk." He answered that he needed time to think. "Just leave me alone," he demanded.

A part of me feared that Jon was having an emotional breakdown. He was trembling and walking rapidly, with a disturbed look in his eyes.

I stopped the car and prayed, "Lord, what should I do?" Then I thought, "Well, Lord, maybe he does need to be alone."

I went home, calmed the children and put them to bed. I got out my Bible and began reading and talking to the Lord: "Just take care of Jon. Whatever happens, just take care of him." As I sat there a real peace came over me. At that moment I heard the key turn in the door. I felt the presence and warmth of the Lord, and I continued to pray as Jon came in. "Lord, give me the right words to say. Please, dear God, I love him so much."

Jon came in and slumped into a chair. His body was wringing wet with perspiration. His expression was blank, almost lifeless. I grasped his hand and it went limp. I said, "Please, Jon, talk to me. Let me know you're all right." We sat there for a very long time. He finally said, "All the way home, all sorts of confused things ran through my head, like 'Man, you're really cracking up.' Then I'd tell myself, 'No, no, you're just tired,' and on and on."

We sat up the whole night talking about our marriage, his drinking, and God. It was a time of renewal for us. For the first time Jon responded positively about Christ. He wanted to hear. It was beautiful. What seemed at first to be a disaster turned out to be a precious, sweet time, a real sharing of our selves.

Not long after that night I noticed a change in my husband. He began attending church with me occasionally. God began to tenderly deal with Jon as he heard the Word. He began taking more interest in our home and the children. He began to stay home more, and as his desire to take care of us increased he decided he wanted to take the children to church every Sunday.

A peace slowly began to settle over our home and over Jon. He became more responsible, and although he was still drinking I watched his drinking gradually decrease.

As Jon's eyes and mind began to clear, he began to see himself and his "friends" as they really were. He saw how their drinking was destroying most of them physically, and destroying their homes.

Only a few months passed before Jon personally asked Jesus Christ into his life.

God not only restored our marriage, but He matured us and made our relationship better than it ever was before. Christ has made our in-law relationship more pleasant, more loving, by our letting Him love them through us. Although our relationship with Jesus Christ hasn't yet been shared by our parents, we are praying that it will be and that we will all be united in heaven with our Lord.

About one year ago while attending a neighborhood Bible study I began to listen to Darien Cooper's tape series on God's role for a woman entitled, "Will the Real Woman Please Stand Up?" As we listened to a tape a week, we also used her book, *You Can Be the Wife of a Happy Husband,* as reference material. I felt like shouting with glee that such a book was available for women. I was excited because only through trial and error had I found the principles she shares so clearly in the tapes and the book. I thought how wonderful it was that other women wouldn't have to travel the same treacherous road I had. Here are the principles directly from God's Word for every woman, and I know from experience that they work!

Our quiet talks and long walks together have become a reality once again. Occasionally we visit my folks and again stroll along those Miami beaches hand in hand. Everything is so different now.

We sit silently watching the sun set over the restless sea. So many tides have rolled in and returned, so many storms have lashed the sea . . . and some ships have been swamped by turbulent waves while others returned to port safely—like ours.

Our voyage was launched at one port, has battled the storms of life, and now rests in the harbor with treasures from afar. God has repaired and deepened our love. As I relaxed in the tranquil strength of Jon's arms, I felt the last ray of sunlight on my face and I thanked God for giving us another precious day. And yet our real voyage has just begun.

Reminiscing with Darien:

Wednesday morning was here! My mind touched on the fact that my Tuesday class was over and my Thursday class was a day ahead. Today would be free to tie up some loose ends around my home.

About 10:30 I'd just cut shelf paper and gotten all the cans out of the kitchen cabinets when the phone rang. My heart sank as a voice said, "Mrs. Cooper, weren't you supposed to hold a question-and-answer session for our Bible class at ten o'clock today?"

Oh, no! How could I have made such a mistake? There was no excuse. I simply had not consulted my calendar in several days and this engagement had slipped my mind.

The class had just concluded its ten-week tape course on "The Real Woman." Fortunately, there were two tapes on child training they still hadn't heard, and they graciously agreed to put on a tape while I dressed and rushed over.

God, in His marvelous grace, once again used my blundering for good. As I apologized to the group for my mistake, one woman said she wouldn't have been there had I not been late as her car had broken down. Another confided how comforting it was to know that I made mistakes just like everyone else. I was tempted to take several hours and comfort her some more!

Often when I've failed I think, "Lord, I'll never teach women again. I'm still too big of a mess myself." Then I am reminded that it's God's truths which are life-changing and perfect, not me. None of us will be perfect until Jesus takes us to be with Him.

As we ate lunch, a woman asked me if I had any experience counseling women whose husbands were alcoholics. When I explained that my contact with such situations had been limited, Doanne began to share what God had done in her marriage.

Through a friend Doanne had learned that I would be in Newnan for this session and she had driven from Montgomery,

Alabama. I was so impressed by Doanne's testimony that I asked her to prepare it for this book.

Doanne emphasized that the key ingredient to living successfully with an alcoholic husband was to accept him as he is and to consistently manifest Christ's love. She had tried complaining, nagging, and threatening, to no avail. Obviously Jon had a dual conflict: problems for which he had found no answers, and situations that facilitated his drinking. The liquor bottle became Jon's pleasant diversion and his route of escape.

Doanne's criticism only added to the problem. God reminds us how painful it is to live with a complaining wife: "It is better to dwell in a corner of the housetop [on the flat oriental roof, exposed to all kinds of weather] than in a house shared with a nagging, quarrelsome *and* faultfinding woman" (Prov. 21:9, AMP).

Before Doanne became a Christian, she did not have the power within her to cope with such problems. Even as a new Christian, she complicated the problem by not understanding the message in 1 Peter 3:1-2, where God reminds a Christian wife that her non-Christian husband may be won to Christ through her chaste and respectful behavior. When Doanne refused to go certain places with Jon, he felt he had been abandoned in preference for a stranger. Had she looked at the situation from Jon's viewpoint, she would have realized that he felt threatened, rejected, and afraid that he was losing her. Lacking spiritual insight, Jon could not understand Doanne's actions (1 Cor. 2:14).

Doanne finally realized that being an understanding, confident wife was the real way to share Jesus with Jon. Rather than "falling apart" over this or being fearful of that, she needed to evidence calm strength and quenchless love stemming from assurance that her future was in God's control. The beauty of a peaceful spirit, together with Doanne's praise for Jon's good traits and her response to his leadership, set the stage for God to draw Jon to Himself. She helped also.

Doanne learned not to take Jon's ugly behavior personally

when she was not at fault. She was regularly studying God's Word and correcting areas that He showed her needed changing. That was all God expected of her. Jon's irritability could be explained by unresolved conflicts in other areas of his life. Her response to Jon was to comfort and encourage him, rather than adding to the problem by being offended.

Today Jon is a Christian. Doanne had the opportunity to share biblical truths with him when he began to seek answers. She was careful, however, to answer only what he asked about and not to turn him off by sharing too much. She would share with any Christian that the way to contentment and victory in any need is in doing everything "as unto the Lord" (Col. 3:17, 23). It's not easy, but it's glorious.

Thinking Through with You:

Question:*What encouragement and guidance does God give for winning a non-Christian husband to the Lord?*
Answer: "Wives, be submissive to your own husbands so that even if any of them are disobedient to the Word, they may be won without a word by the behavior of their wives, as they observe your chaste and respectful behavior" (1 Peter 3:1–2, NASB).

Q.: *How can you be a relaxed wife when marital storms swirl around you?*
A.: "Let Him have all your worries and cares, for He is always thinking about you and watching everything that concerns you" (1 Peter 5:7, LB).

Q.: *What is the power of temperate, kind speech?*
A.: "A soft answer turns away wrath; but grievous words stir up anger" (Prov. 15:1, AMP). "By long forbearing and calmness of spirit, a judge or ruler is persuaded, and soft speech breaks down the most bonelike resistance" (Prov. 25:15, AMP.).

6

Depression Doesn't Live Here Anymore

April Harrell

Blackness hung like an immovable veil over me. I struggled to open my eyes, to reach into the conscious world. *Where am I?* My eyes opened to an unfamiliar room. Sterile white walls surrounded me. I fought desperately to clear the confusion, the gaze engulfing my mind.

The pills. I had taken the whole bottle.

What am I doing here? I'm supposed to be dead! "Dear God," I cried, "can't I even kill myself?" Tears of anguish washed down my face. Living or dying, both seemed impossible tasks for me. As my thoughts shrank back behind the black veil, the "whys," the events that had brought me to today, flashed through my recollections like a high-speed movie. Where had it all begun?

I recalled high school, 1956, a lifetime away. My world then had been filled with school, parties, and dates. Being elected homecoming queen had been the culmination of my junior year.

I had learned early the road to popularity: I was a "people-pleaser," par excellence. Even at that point in my life, my real self was torn between the sweet, apple-pie April whom everyone knew, and the swinging, rebellious April that few people met. The two irreconcilable presonalities, "Good April" and "Bad April," already had begun their separate lives. During my senior year a boy named Keith joined my math class. I sat for an entire period gazing at him, mentally bidding him to turn around and look at me. He didn't.

At home that afternoon I stared into the mirror. My tall, slender frame had filled out well. My honey blonde hair hung down in soft waves around my shoulders. I tried on this dress and that, finally deciding on a white sweater and matching tight skirt.

"That ought to get his attention," I thought. It did.

Keith was tall and handsome, with flashing green eyes, set off by a silhouette of light-brown hair. His spirited personality had won him instant admiration and helped him to be voted "most popular" boy in our senior class.

Keith was everything I dreamed I had ever wanted, and I meant to have him. With graduation behind us, visions of marriage loomed immediately ahead on my horizon. With Keith in agreement, I called our church minister to discuss our wedding plans.

He began to explain the sanctity of marriage, but I didn't hear much—I was thinking of the fun of marriage. He spoke of a lasting commitment to each other, and I answered with exaggerated respect: "Dr. Howell, I really understand that."

In reality, I understood hardly anything. I wanted Keith exclusively. I wanted him right away. What else was important?

White carnations and green ivy adorned the church in Green Bay that warm September day. The beautiful notes of "Because" drifted through the church as Mama put the finishing touches on my gown.

As I stepped into the aisle, I saw Keith waiting for me at the altar, a confident, loving smile lighting his face. Excitement so filled my heart that it seemed like someone else repeating those vows. I knew there could never be another day so beautiful as this.

As the routine of marriage settled in, the starry glamor of first love began to fade into normalcy. Honeymoons were sup-

posed to last forever, I thought. I wasn't prepared for reality.
I did my best to be a good wife. I loved Keith very much.
To me, he was everything good and perfect in this world, and
deep inside I knew he was everything I wasn't.

Keith spent the next few years working hard to get a foot-
hold in the bridge-building industry. In time he was made a
supervisor. I became aware there were rivers all over the world,
and it seemed that Keith was building bridges over all of them!
He traveled extensively and for long periods of time.

Left at home, an aching syndrome of loneliness beset me.
I wasn't the kind of woman to exist without male companionship and attention, and a fire began to burn in my soul. Love
Keith as I did, "Bad April" responded more and more to the
attraction of other men.

I tried to relieve my frustrations with housework, reading
and neighborhood activities—bridge with the girls, lunch at
the country club. I managed to control the war inside during
the day, but at night the demons of loneliness and sensuality
reared their ugly heads.

I didn't know how to handle these desires. They seemed as
much a part of the real me as my love for Keith. Though I
had professed faith in Christ in my early teens, I considered
Christianity more as a way to get into heaven than a way of
living. Torn by fervent longings with my husband far away, I
surrendered to illicit relationships. Keith never knew.

The years passed and Keith was successful in business. We
had three healthy children, but I was getting sick. Never able
to appease the counterparts of my inner self, I became frustrated, depressed and neurotic.

My mind played tricks on me. Reality became an illusion.
Details of my carnal relationships burned in my eyes, and at
times I wasn't sure whether I had sinned against God or was
deluded by fantasy. Ordinary mistakes swelled to horrid crimes
which tormented my soul.

Soon dressing myself each morning became a major ac-
complishment. One day began to melt into the next. Activities
around me faded in and out of existence. Fatigue hung heavy

but I couldn't relax. I couldn't sleep. "Bad April," "Good April," sins, sex, confusion. Finally I couldn't stand another day.

In a flight of desperation I entered a sanitarium in Madison. As I walked up the steps, I reached out for the last help I could think of. Hoping He'd hear, I prayed, "Dear God, please give me a Christian counselor."

The Lord answered my prayer. He provided a dear Christian woman for counseling. She visited me almost every day, but my twisted mind couldn't comprehend the real answers to my problems.

My small room at the sanitarium, with its locked door, kept the fears and pressures of life outside. A sense of security came like a warm blanket to my days. Every moment of my day was arranged; personal decisions were not necessary. Like a child I followed orders, and obedience brought special privileges.

Daily counseling plus group therapy was the basis of my treatment. "Group" problems, like so much garbage, were spewed out while 15 people who couldn't figure their way out of paper bags offered their in-depth thoughts and advice!

No solutions were found to my deep inner turmoil. No major problems were solved. Yet, rested and tranquilized, I began to cope with life. Three months passed, and the doctors decided it was time for my release. The thought of home panicked me. The hospital was my haven. They couldn't take me away from the only peace I'd found!

Only through being deceived did I agree to leave. I was told I'd have to take a month's outside leave and then I could return. In retrospect, I realize I copped out in running to the hospital—a "breakdown" was socially acceptable when one couldn't cope with life.

Keith picked me up and took me home. After a few weeks, family obligations outweighed my need to run, so life went on as before: one step forward, two steps back; two steps forward, one step back.

So the next six years went. There were times when I'd yearn

for spiritual fulfillment. I read the Bible and prayed. I'd try to trust God, but my flimsy faith never allowed me to entrust myself to Him rather than to pills.

By 1972 my precarious grip on life was slipping. I was losing hope. Depression streaked my days. Destructive self-pity ate at my resolves.

Keith decided it would be more profitable for him to move south. Atlanta seemed like the logical choice since Keith's company had a large office there.

Our relationship had become more and more strained, though I couldn't discern the reason. I realized how mixed up I was, but Keith's edgy restlessness was a mystery.

He called one evening and said, "April, let's just forget it. You do your thing, and I'll do mine. I'm going ahead with my move to Atlanta."

Hysterically I yelled, "Not on your life! I'm moving out of this town. I don't care what happens to you and me, but I'm getting these kids out of here and we will have to see how it goes from there."

I associated Green Bay, my home for 33 years, with my problems. I wanted to get away from the small town where I felt everyone knew everyone else's business. I wanted to run again.

Ice floated in the Fox River and snow lay on the ground when we left Green Bay. When we arrived in Atlanta, the dogwoods were just beginning to blossom. For a short time I thought that perhaps our lives also would bloom again.

There were days when, after a hard day of housecleaning, Keith would deliver a sharp criticism and I would collapse in despair. I was so dependent on Keith's words of approval. Everything I did was to please him. What he thought and said could make or destroy my day.

The pressure drove me down and down. Our conflicts came to a head shortly after we moved to Atlanta and Keith packed up and left home. He moved in with an assistant who lived in Decatur.

A few weeks passed, then because of a myriad of circumstances and the illness of our children, I had to call Keith. During the conversation he asked me, "Are you asking me to come home?" I answered, "Yes, Keith, you belong here."

It was settled, or was it? No problems had been discussed, or solutions found; just a decision made.

Depression seemed my constant companion. The black veil was beginning to fall. I knew what was going on around me: my eyes saw, my ears heard, yet it was rather like watching a play in which I no longer could or cared to participate. Loneliness oppressed me. I was locked behind a door, one I constructed myself.

I tried to tell Keith, and I tried to tell my friends how I felt, what I feared and the needs I had, but I don't think anyone understood. Between my speaking and their hearing, the pain behind the words got lost.

"I don't even care anymore," I thought. "It really doesn't matter. There is no way to undo all the mistakes, all the rottenness; no way to forget the pain; no one to understand . . . I need a pill."

Opening the drawer, I found my lovely collection. Pills, two lovely yellow ones, one sky blue one—each containing sweet peace—quiet, soft, floating peace. They offered me a serene world where pain never entered, nor joy, nor tears—a beautiful world of nothingness.

At times I would scream inside: *"Help me. Oh, please, can't you see? Look at me, I'm dying inside. Look at me!"* But my silent screams went unheard.

At church one night I asked the elders to call a prayer meeting for me. I told them that my marriage was in shambles, that I didn't know what the problem was. "I need your prayers," I told them.

Tears fell on my hands as I stared at the floor and began to ask for divine intervention: "I pray that all human frailties be removed and only God's love be present. My marriage is at an end. I can't take it anymore. I don't even know what it is I can't take; I just can't take any more. I'm a Christian, but I seem to find no answers. Please, please pray for my whole family. I don't know where we're headed, but we need prayer."

I felt a measure of peace as I drove home that night. Perhaps the Lord was strengthening me for the heartbreak ahead, but I continued to rely on myself.

When I got home, Keith told me that an old friend of ours from Green Bay was in town. I called her and we agreed to meet at her hotel.

As Jackie talked, my unsolved problems became the topic of conversation. The pain began to spill out. "Jackie," I said, "my marriage is at an end. I don't know what is wrong. If there is anything you know that would help me, please tell me. I don't even know what I am fighting."

She didn't say much for a while, but in time she told me a story which, had it come from anyone else, I would have called a lie. "April, you might as well know what you are up against. Keith has been having affairs for years," she said.

By the time she told me about woman number eight, I said, "Hush, I don't want to hear any more. I can't grasp what I've heard."

The rest of the night was spent in Jackie's hotel room. I couldn't face Keith.

Keith had been my idol. He was good. He was the only guy in the world I trusted. He had always been first in my life, despite my past unfaithfulness. I suppose I actually worshiped him. My idol had fallen. The pain was overwhelming.

I had felt for a long time that there was a barrier between the Lord and me. At that moment I realized it was Keith: he instead of God had been first in my thoughts, first in my love.

I had prayed for years: "Lord, remove whatever is number one, if it is not You!" Now it was done.

When I returned home I confronted Keith with the truth I had learned. He didn't deny it. In my heart I had longed that he would.

Anger rose in his face and voice. "Why in the world did you have to drag all this out?" he asked. I began to realize that he was only upset because I had changed the status quo in our relationship. Momentarily I wished I hadn't.

I still cared so much for Keith that I was determined not to lose him. Like a "good Christian," I tried to "forgive and forget," but not knowing how to appropriate Christ's power, I failed miserably. I tried to suppress my true feelings. I kept the bitterness, the hurt, the hatred locked inside me. There were times when emotions got the best of me and "Bad April" took over, making me act like a raving maniac.

"And you're supposed to be a Christian!" Keith would scoff. "Is this how a Christian acts?"

I looked everywhere for answers. I read current self-help books. I searched for someone who understood the agony of my life. Through Christian books on marriage, I learned how to be an attractive woman; I learned some useful directions and ideas, but nothing life-changing. I kept searching for some Christian woman to whom I could relate, but found none.

Things in our home went from bad to worse. Grief and resentment ate at my soul until I could no longer contain it. I had been popping pills like candy for years—Valium was my best friend. One Saturday the pain of life became too much. I consumed half a bottle of the tranquilizer by afternoon, and when I dopily awoke the next morning I groped my way into the kitchen. Holding onto the counter, I reached into the cabinet and took out a glass. Turning the water on, I filled the glass and reached into my pocket for my pills. I poured out a handful and swallowed them.

Sleep. Sweet nothingness . . . that was my goal.

A bottle of another tranquilizer sat in the cabinet, and I reached for it. In my daze I don't know how much I consumed. I almost crawled back to the bedroom—I didn't want the kids to find me passed out on the floor, but I did want Keith to find me and have the shock hit him, hurt him.

What if the pills don't work?" my groggy mind contemplated. Crawling now, I struggled to reach Keith's shotgun in the closet. Clothes fell everywhere until my hand touched metal. I dragged the gun out and pulled myself back to bed . . . .

The hospital's sterile walls greeted me as my mind pushed aside the black veil, and I returned to consciousness. I realized I had been on a flashback trip through years of hell. I looked around, ran my hands down the rough white sheets and over my body. No bandages, no bullet wounds. I guessed I must have passed out before I could use the gun.

In the next few days I decided my presence at home caused me and everyone else pain and turmoil. I concluded my family would be better off without me. I knew I needed rest, and I needed time to find answers to the problems that beset me.

A doctor at the hospital had told me that I wasn't cut out to be a mother and a wife, that what I wanted was to be a "woman of the world." "Get out," he advised; "it's the best thing you can do for everyone." Still depending on human guidance, I followed his advice. When those hospital doors closed behind me, I walked out on my husband and my children.

I checked into a local motel and looked up a young woman named Manya whom I had met recently, a waitress at a nearby restaurant.

Manya sensed something was wrong, and I spilled my story to her. She had been divorced for a number of years and seemed to understand my confusion.

"You can't stay in a motel forever," she said. "Why don't you come over to my apartment?"

I needed a friend, I needed to feel wanted and I needed someone to talk to, so I accepted Manya's gracious offer.

Keith accepted my absence calmly. He kept in touch by telephone, but I didn't see him or the children. I spent my days job-hunting, without success, until I swallowed my pride and went to work as a waitress with Manya.

I was beginning to find some semblance of peace. I couldn't imagine what my future would be, but I was trying not to think about it too much. One day at a time. I tried to take it slow and easy.

One day I called home to check on the children. My mother-in-law answered, and we chatted for a few minutes about news of the children. She told me that Keith had been taking them to church, an innovation that I found hard to believe. Something troubled me about our conversation. I had intended for Keith to bear the full responsibility for the children's care; I didn't want an outsider running my home.

I was being torn again. What should I do?

Suddenly I felt as if I had committed the ultimate sin: I, the mother, had left my children and my husband.

With a shaking hand, I dialed my home. "Mom," I told her, "I know I have made lots of mistakes. I have failed everyone, but I'm coming home."

When Manya came in that evening, I told her of my decision. "I don't know if what I am doing is any more right than what I have done in the past, but I have to go home," I said. "I'll never forget that you were there when I really needed a friend."

"April," she said, "just remember that my door is always open if you ever need a place to stay or just to talk. You take care when you get home and see if you can't get things off on the right foot this time."

Keith was out of town when I walked back into my home. I picked up where I had left off. No solutions, no new directions were visible. I still leaned on tranquilizers to stabilize my emotions.

One afternoon I was standing in the kitchen when I heard Keith's car in the driveway. Automatically I tightened up inside. I wasn't sure what his reaction to my coming home would be. I soon found out. He opened the door and gently took me in his arms.

Things around our house slowly began to change. Little things: his verbal denunciations stopped, and compliments were more frequent. Apparently, in part, my silent screams for help were finally being answered. And slowly I began to realize that I had always heard only the negative. I had never listened for the good. I had been so strung-out that I had overreacted.

Keith and I began to be more honest with each other. This

took a great effort on my part. I began to let him know, without nagging, when his words hurt. This mutual caring, in place of accusations, was a totally new experience for me.

Life was better, but my problems and confusion were not ended. I knew I must learn to live one day at a time—to handle and confront only today's problems and not to concern myself with the "what ifs" of tomorrow—but it was hard. Not until a few months later would I learn how to have a moment-by-moment relationship with Jesus Christ that enabled me to depend on Him, not on myself. And not until then did I realize that I had been trying to program God, to fit Him into my plans, just as I had done with everyone else. I also discovered that God's ways are not my ways. "There is a way that seems right to a man and appears straight before him, but at the end of it are the ways of death" (Prov. 16:25, AMP.).

While doing volunteer work at my church, I first heard of Darien Cooper from my neighbor, Barbara McIntire. "April, I just know this is what you have been looking for, the answers you need. Won't you please go with me when the seminars begin again?" she pled.

"Well, Barbara, we'll see," I'd say, procrastinating.

Barbara lent the tapes of the classes to me and I listened while I worked. I thought Darien Cooper was crazy! There wasn't a name in the book I didn't call her. "She doesn't understand my situation," I fumed. If she were walking in my shoes, she'd change her story. About halfway through the taped course, I picked up the recorder in frustration and threw it across the room. "Who in the world does she think she is?" I screamed.

The solution was plain to me: "Just remove all these problems," I prayed continually, "and I won't be up-tight." Yet I began to feel as if He were saying, "April, I want to teach you through your problems. I want you to grow, to become strong, to become the woman I created you to be."

As my search continued I joined a prayer group in my neighborhood which turned out to be a Darien Cooper "fan club." I admitted to them that I couldn't accept the things Mrs. Cooper was teaching.

Months later a girl who was new to the group, Reba, brought me a book she said I ought to read. It was *You Can Be The Wife of a Happy Husband,* by Darien Cooper. I thanked her and reluctantly took the book. I prayed, "Lord, I will read this book, but You're going to have to change my attitude. I'm willing, but it is up to You."

About this time I heard of another Cooper seminar. Members of the prayer group began to pray for a change in my attitude so I would attend.

I wanted my marriage to work. I knew my attitudes and actions at home were still wrong. I knew that real changes had to take place for any lasting improvements. I began to feel that maybe the principles taught by Darien Cooper might be the answers I was looking for.

The day came for the class and I did something totally out of character for me: I went alone. I didn't call anyone; I didn't ask for emotional support.

Even though our lives were different, I identified with Anne Carroll the moment she began to speak to the class. I had never seen such complete transformation in a woman. I had never met anyone who had made the transition from the "swinging life" to real-life Christianity. It was Anne who convinced me that a whole new life was possible, even for me. It took both Anne and Darien to make the seminar complete for me.

I knew that I could talk with these women, that they would understand. There would be no criticism, only love, through Christ.

As I attended the seminar, I realized that I hadn't been rebelling against Darien Cooper's ideas. These were *God's* principles, straight out of the Bible. Darien had just given the time, energy and love to allow God to use her.

When I first heard Darien speak, among my thoughts were: "She really has it all together."

But no one can identify with perfection and slowly I began

to see that she too was human. She revealed her mistakes to us. I was fascinated that she was still learning. She made me feel so much better about myself.

After class one morning, I told Darien how Keith's infidelity had almost destroyed me. Nothing had seemed to help, and I kept asking my prayer group to pray that I would completely forget Keith's sin.

"In that act alone, April," Darien said, "it is obvious that you have not really forgiven Keith. You haven't been willing to forget, so obviously you haven't really forgiven. You have kept the memories alive by constantly keeping the subject before you, by constantly discussing it with the prayer group and others."

Darien continued: "The way to forget is not to recall the act to your offender, not to tell it to others, and not to allow yourself to dwell upon it. April, the moment it comes to your mind, you should thank God that He has taken care of it, and respond rightly to Keith, letting God remove it from your mind."

She shared with me many Scriptures to reinforce the solution she had given.

The love that Keith and I once knew had not returned. But as I learned what true love is, I began to take my rightful place as Keith's helpmate. He became the head of our household. In giving myself to him, I realized that love acts for the happiness of others, not for its own. And like a seed, the old love that I had known began to grow again in my heart. Now I could more fully comprehend the words: "For where your treasure is, there your heart will be also" (Matt 6:21, NIV).

I am enjoying so many little things I never cared for in the past. I have canned 200 jars of vegetables for my family. Just the act of washing the corn and scraping the carrots became an act of love. My bonus came when Keith proudly arranged the jars on a display shelf in our basement den and said, "You are something else; I am so very proud of you. It is really a pleasure to come home now."

I glowed all over. What a difference! "Thank you; you have

no idea how much fulfillment I'm getting from so many small things."

I have learned how to take one day at a time. After years of popping pills, I have kicked the habit through the power of Jesus Christ. I don't mean that I have conquered all my problems, And when I get my eyes off the Lord and decide that a problem is one I can handle, I fall flat on my face.

At a drug clinic, a doctor explained that one of the drugs I had been taking was physically addictive. Though I had experienced withdrawal symptoms, I had not considered my pills "drugs." I had been much more aware of the sins and weaknesses of hard-drug users than my own.

Now I know the truth about the pills, the truth about myself and truth about Christ. As Jesus said, "So if the Son liberates you . . . then you are really and unquestionably free" (John 8:36, AMP).

The beautiful music of laughter now rings in our home; honest laughter. Love has been renewed. The children are growing in our love and the love of the Lord. When I place dishes in the dishwasher, I thank the Lord and remember the time when I didn't have one. When I wash the clothes, I think of the child who will be wearing them. When I make our bed, I thank God for the love He restored and the good times in that bed.

Someone once gave me a quote by D. L. Moody which has been especially meaningful to me. I make it personal by inserting my name. It goes like this:

"The world has yet to see what God will do with April, for April, and through April, and in April, by April, when she is fully consecrated to Him; I, April, will try my utmost to be that woman."

I thought long and hard about sharing my story with Anne so she could write it. I prayed and discussed it with Keith. It hurt. It isn't easy for me, even now, to admit how sinful my life had been. Exposing the mistakes and the stupidity to the world is difficult.

God reminded me how I had searched Christan books for

someone to identify with, some woman who had come through the depths of depression caused by sin and enabled to walk with Christ. I thought: "Maybe some other woman needs to identify, needs to know that there is hope, that there are answers." Keith said to go ahead with our story, so I did.

My prayer is:

"Dear God, please use these words, the pain, the sin and the solutions to help others. Impress readers' hearts with the truth that there is no sin, no problem, no failure which You can't forgive. Touch the heart of that woman whose only way of survival is to meet each day, each problem with a pill or a drink. Truly let her know how wonderful it is to be "free" and that Christ can do it if only she will let Him.

"Speak to the heart of that woman who thinks, because the feeling of love has faded from her marriage, that divorce is the answer. Show her what real love is and how You can so gloriously restore a love thought dead. For the woman lost behind the black veil of depression, encourage her. May Your Spirit witness to her. And may this story let her know that truly Christ can remove that veil forever. This is my prayer in Jesus Christ's name, Amen."

Reminiscing with Darien:

April's eyes sparkled as I explained that Anne and I were searching for women who would share their testimonies for this book. She blurted out almost before I finished talking that she had been waiting for an opportunity to tell the world what Christ had done in her life. As time passed, April wasn't sure that she would be able to write her testimony. Going into the dark recesses of her mind was painful and frustrating. I reassured her that God would not ask her to do anything unless He provided the necessary strength. When the time came, she and Anne were able to work together to present her story. I appreciate her willingness to share her successes and failures in order that others may be encouraged to trust Christ.

April's turmoil-filled life could be summarized by the Apostle Paul's words: "I don't understand myself at all, for I really want to do what is right, but I can't. I do what I don't want to—what I hate. . . . I love to do God's will so far as my new nature is concerned; but there is something else deep within me, in my lower nature, that is at war with my mind and wins the fight and makes me a slave to the sin that is still within me. In my mind I want to be God's willing servant, but instead I find myself still enslaved to sin. So you see how it is: my new life tells me to do right, but the old nature that is still inside me loves to sin. Oh, what a terrible predicament I'm in! Who will free me from my slavery to this deadly lower nature? Thank God! It has been done by Jesus Christ, our Lord. He has set me free" (Rom. 7:15, 22-25, LB).

For many years April was enslaved to her old nature because she did not know to confess her sins and to allow Christ to control her life as she established right patterns of living.

April slowly began to see that her wrong responses to the pressures and responsibilities of life had led her deeper and deeper into the endless spiral of depression. She had tried to make Keith meet needs in her life that only Jesus Christ could meet. When he couldn't fill this impossible role, she responded with resentment and bitterness. She reacted with jealousy toward Keith's freedom from the home responsibilities that were so burdensome for her. She tried to fill her loneliness and need for companionship with illicit relations. April's sinful reaction to her initial problems had violated the principles in God's Word that were designed to protect her. God described through Jeremiah the inevitable results: "Your ways and your doings have brought these things down upon you; this is your calamity and doom; surely it is bitter, for surely it reaches your very heart" (Jer. 4:18, AMP.).

The only way April knew to deal with her problems was to increase the amount of drugs she was taking. But drugs could not suppress the anguish caused by Keith's infidelity. Her attempted suicide, as well as her walking out on her children and husband, was an act of vengeance toward them.

When April confided the nasty names she had called me, I remembered how I had rebelled when I first heard the truths I later shared with others. I know how painful it is to see one's rottenness. Yet God shows us our actual condition so we will trust Him to make the necessary changes in our lives.

Because April's depression was a result of sin in her life, there was hope for her. She learned to reverse the cycle that had plunged her into depression by the following steps:

1. Admit your wrong response or action is sin against God.
2. Confess your sin to God, according to 1 John 1:9.
3. Accept God's promised forgiveness.
4. Focus your thoughts on Christ's sufficiency for your particular situation.
5. Take appropriate steps to avoid repeating the same failures.
6. Thank God that He will give you strength to trust Him throughout your struggle.

These steps will work for any woman who truly wants her life to be new and fulfilling.

Thinking Through with You:

Question: *How can Christians overcome the sinful influence of the continuing "old nature" within us?*
Answer: "Walk by the Spirit, and you will not carry out the desire of the flesh. For the flesh sets its desire against the Spirit, and the Spirit against the flesh, for these are in opposition to one another, so that you may not do the things that you please. . . . Now the deeds of the flesh are evident, which are immorality . . . idolatry . . . outbursts of anger . . . drunkenness . . . But the fruit of the Spirit is love, joy, peace, patience, kindness, goodness, faithfulness, gentleness, self-control. . . ." (Gal. 5:16-17, 19-23, NASB).

Q.: *After his own failures and acceptance of forgiveness, how did the Apostle Peter affirm God's faithfulness?*
A.: "He who believes in Him—who adheres to, trusts in and relies on Him—shall never be disappointed or put to shame" (1 Peter 2:6, AMP.).

Q.: *How far is our forgiveness of others to reach?*
A.: "As those who have been chosen of God . . . put on a heart of compassion . . . bearing with one another, and forgiving each other . . . just as the Lord forgave you, so also should you" (Col. 3:12-13, NASB).

Q.: *How do we know that good feelings are to be a product rather than the source of right actions?*
A.: "Joy fills hearts that are planning for good!" (Prov. 12:20, LB).

7

"Keep Those Trucks Coming, Mack!"

Janice Bruner

There was a rainbow touching the earth on our way home. I looked at it hopefully: this was the first sign of color in our whole honeymoon!

I was bewildered—how could anyone be so disappointed with a honeymoon?

All my life I had considered myself a colorful person. I had always felt the admiration of friends my own age and older people as well. In high school, I was Miss This and Miss That. I had skipped hardly any of the bright lights.

My long, dark hair, blue eyes and outgoing personality fascinated my steady boyfriend, Rod, to a point where he would do anything to please me. I'd complain, "Rod always asks me where we should go and what we should do. I just wish he'd make the decisions and tell me where we're going."

Later at college and during my nursing career, I continued to reap attention. When I met Brad, the tables were turned as I found myself caring more for him than he cared for me! All too often he made decisions that ignored me. I didn't like that either!

My unrest dissolved when I met Mack. He was my idea of a knight in shining armor, six-foot-two, dark and handsome, and altogether different from Rod, Brad, or any other fellow I had dated. Mack became all I ever wanted, and it was like a story in a book when he told me that he wanted me too. Our beautiful wedding followed—and then the disappointing honeymoon.

I tried not to think about it. Instead I forced myself to think of the dream house where we would live and have a perfect marriage. The house, which Mack's father had given us, would make everything turn out right, I thought.

Then we arrived! And I could not believe my eyes! Was this old house what Mack had described in glowing terms? Or had my romantic heart just heard it that way?

In my dreams rainbows arched over honeymoon cottages that had groceries in clean cabinets, gingham at the windows, geraniums in window boxes and warm rugs to dig your toes into. But, oh, the reality: cracked walls, accumulated junk, roaches, and a toilet that couldn't be repaired and had to be thrown out the second-story window!

For three years our "dream house" remained bare, unremodeled, and stale. The little improvements I made were hardly noticeable as the house was in need of such major repairs. I would come home from my nursing job, walk numbly through the door, and drop my savings alongside my husband's in our next dream-house fund.

Talking about the problems didn't solve anything for me. Mack loved to discuss our situation, always optimistically. I dreaded the encounters because it's very difficult for me to discuss my feelings. Things will be different, he'd say, if I only met his needs. "What needs?" I'd ask. I wanted desperately to please, but all he ever asked was things like, "Go to the lumber yard and buy some nails"; "Bring me the hammer"; or "Mend my pants." Big deal!

When I'd forget to run one of his errands, he'd be impatient. "Why don't you make a list," he suggested. "Make a list," became fighting words to me. Why should I start each day making a list of things to do for him when my needs were not being met? I wanted Mack to be proud of me—to think I was extra-special—and I felt like I was drowning in trivia—all five-foot-three of me.

Our frustrations faded into the background when we moved into the grand house we had schemed and saved to build. We had designed "just what we always wanted," we thought. I didn't get window boxes, but I did manage custom-made shutters, wallpaper, a lush lawn, one rose bush, doorbells—and heartaches. The roaches didn't accompany us to our new house, but the bugs in my old self did.

They showed up in various places. There was the drapery rod that came out of the wall and hung from one end for a year. Some women might have called a repairman, but I didn't need to because my talented husband could fix anything (if he wanted to).

After going around the mulberry bush with him, nagging, pleading, coaxing and loving, then back to nagging again, I finally became bitter about dangling curtain rods and other loose ends. If Mack really loved me, he'd see how much these things meant to me and fix them!

After months of turmoil, he fixed the defect. Just like that, but it didn't mean anything to me. By then I'd struggled so long that I was emotionally exhausted. A new house had not met my needs. What was the answer?

As Darien Cooper's sister, I had grown up eight years her junior. I'd always viewed Darien as an ideal sister, smart and logical. She was more aggressive than I, and openly derived pleasure from mastering her problems. I labeled myself as "passive" and "just different" because I didn't like to talk through my problems. That always got too personal and took too much time; I kept my problems to myself—until the pressure valve exploded in a crying session.

Living in Orlando, we visited Darien and her family about every three months. As my marital problems became more baffling, I began to view our visits as my pressure-valve release. With Darien prodding, I would tearfully divulge the woe engulfing at least one major problem. We would talk it through and I'd go home, red-eyed, with a new-found principle from the Bible to put into practice. My soul would seem sore for about two weeks after each visit—I'm sure I was using certain spiritual muscles for the first time!

Slowly, from God's Word, I began to see my real self: ugly. I didn't like that. The brilliant colors of my "self-portrait" went glimmering and the true, cloudy outlines revealed my impatient, proud, and bitter profile.

I began to see that Mack needed a helpmate who was available; he needed my participation in the "little things." I should consider his needs when planning my day, and be available for what he liked to do when he came home from work.

Working this out wasn't always what I would have planned. Mack would invite me out to the cold garage, infested with mosquitoes that tortured my legs, to watch him work. Interesting things, like grinding valves or scraping up oil off the concrete floor! Sometimes I'd respond with a nod and bored, "Really?" Other times I was able to put my whole self into my participation.

As the months rolled along, I realized that as I gave myself willingly to my husband, he abundantly gave of himself back to me. If I had to leave the dishes to be with him, he'd help me with them later. A closeness grew that wouldn't have been possible any other way.

It was a new adventure learning that God has designed specific principles for the marriage relationship and that they work. God designed me to respond to Mack in certain ways because He had my best interests at heart. And Jesus Christ was coming alive to me in a new way. I had accepted him as my personal Saviour as a child, but now I was seeing Him as a way of life.

The days that I'd willingly surrender my free time to pick up nuts and bolts, recaps, roofing shingles and lumber in town, I'd invariably have a need of my own met. One day as I ran errands for Mack, I found a much-needed pair of red sandals for two dollars that lasted for three years. Apparently God wanted me to have a long-term reminder of His faithfulness. Another day, when I was riding around town with

Mack, he suggested that we stop at a garage sale—that in itself was phenomenal! We picked up articles that we needed at a fraction of their cost. And we'd enjoyed it together.

I even woke up less grumpy and more agreeable in the mornings. That, definitely, was not the old me! Little did I realize how much chipping and sanding from the old me had to be done to allow the real, new me to emerge.

Darien suggested that God works and leads in our lives through our husbands, and that God was trying to develop patience in my life. I knew I was very impatient and could see the merit in this lesson, but she went on to suggest that my attitude toward Mack revealed my spiritual relationship with Christ. This I couldn't believe. Everything was great between Christ and me; Mack simply was impossible at times.

Shortly afterward I was pulling weeds from my rose bush when Mack asked me to stop and drag the garden hose to a different area of the yard for him. I refused. Why, I reasoned, should I stop my work and do that piddling job for him?

The next day as I was walking to the mailbox, I saw my next-door neighbor working in her yard. The Lord quickened my heart with the thought, "Go talk with Mrs. Jones. Share with her how she can know Me personally." I spontaneously reacted: "I don't want to stop what I'm doing to share with her. Some other time." While returning to the house, I realized that my rejection of Christ's leading was identical to my refusal of my husband's request the day before. I was indeed rebellious toward authority.

God used our first child 'Chelle to teach me more about obedience and trust toward God through my husband.

Mack and I dearly loved 'Chelle. She looked like a little Oriental doll at birth, with jet-black hair and dark eyes. As she grew and developed, sometimes we'd reflect that she had brought us so much joy already that if God took her to heaven we could still be grateful. I was soon to realize that saying those words was much easier than living them.

One day when 'Chelle was a year and a half, we prepared for a trip to town. I would drive the car and Mack was taking the truck to pick up some building supplies. Imagine my horror when Mack put 'Chelle in the back of the pickup truck! Knowing the freedom that Mack had as a child, I was sure he was going to let her ride there alone the eight miles into town along a four-lane highway.

Impetuously I grabbed her up and put in my car. Muscular Mack, in turn, grabbed her back, placed her in the back of the truck and left!

I was sure I'd never see her alive again. I knew I'd been wrong in defying my husband, and I could someday ask his forgiveness, but I didn't want to pay for his bad judgment with the death of our daughter!

I ached so badly inside I couldn't cry hard enough to relieve the pain as I gripped the back door. I felt like I'd been hit by one of those large trucks on the highway, yes, a "Mack truck."

The sofa soaked up my tears, but it didn't help. It was probably only moments, but it seemed an eternity until I looked up and saw Mack at my side, with 'Chelle in his arms. He had never intended for her to ride in the back on the highway—he meant to transfer her to the cab down the road.

Why hadn't I trusted Mack? Why hadn't I trusted God? Why my violent reaction?

The truth resounded in my mind, embarrassingly clear! I did not trust my husband with our daughter; I did not trust God with our daughter. I'd previously experienced fear as I'd watched Mack toss 'Chelle into the air, catching her in play, and his bicycle rides with her had frightened me.

I labeled my worry "motherly concern." It was sin. My masquerade gradually ended over these next four years as God taught me to let 'Chelle go.

One evening when Mack was working late, I heard something outside. My fear swung into full gear, and I fed it until it was robust. I was completely miserable until Mack breezed into the driveway. By that time I was petrified with fear, my stomach ached and my jaws were tight.

The next night I decided I didn't want to go that route

again. I decided to be logical—to think through my problem. "Now, if Mack were here with me I wouldn't be afraid," I reasoned. As clearly as if I'd heard it for the first time, I knew: Either God is here with you or He isn't. Which is it? Does God care for you as carefully as Mack does? You trust Mack—but let's face it, if you really trusted God you wouldn't be afraid. I'd put a limit on God, saying in effect, "You can go pretty far, but not that far."

Then I admitted:

The way I trust my husband is the way I trust the Lord.

The way I respond to my husband is the way I whisper to God.

The way I seek the leadership of my husband is the way I follow my Lord.

The way I plan for my husband is the way I entrust tomorrow to my God.

The way I shout to my husband is the way I scream out at God!

The way I bridle my tongue toward my husband is the way I harness my power from God.

The way I relate to my husband is the way I relate to God.

I was to face other tests as Mack and I put our energies into being good parents.

One day, out of the blue, 'Chelle began stuttering. I had quit work when 'Chelle was born, but I researched my nursing notes and concluded this would pass. Neither of us said much about it at first. Then her stuttering got worse; she stammered with almost every word.

Mack and I had been studying God's Word from Proverbs on raising children. With the help of an able teacher, we began to see the importance of scriptual training. We saw that conquering a child's will in love and consistency was the overall issue confronting us.

Mack decided to put the principle into practice. "We'll discipline her," he said, "because this is simply a bad habit she has developed. Every time she consistently stutters, we'll spank her with the rod."

My responder-signals went berserk. Surely that was all wrong! That would seriously damage her character.

"Oh, dear, I believe I hear another Mack truck roaring toward me," I thought.

Mack was consistent in his discipine. I half-heartedly tried to carry out his orders. While he was at work and 'Chelle and I were at home together, I'd frequently pretend not to hear her stuttering. Or I'd say to myself, "Oh, that was just a little one."

One afternoon when Mack was out plowing the garden and I was cooking supper, 'Chelle started the awfullest case of stuttering I ever heard. I was consciously trusting Christ to be my patience and wisdom, but suddenly I didn't think I could stand it anymore. I escaped to the bathroom to pray. But the same old grinding questions came up: "Do you really trust Mack? What if he's wrong?" My fear revealed that I wasn't trusting. I reassured myself, "Either God is limited or He isn't."

When Mack came in, 'Chelle virtually stopped stuttering. I thought, "What goes here? What am I doing wrong?"

Later, while I washed the dishes, Mack volunteered to give 'Chelle her bath. They had a heart-to-heart talk that I hope goes on forever. He asked her why she stuttered.

"Because I want to, Daddy," she said.

In his firm, kind voice he explained to her, "Honey, God made you in a very special way. If you stutter just because you want to, some day when you get older and bigger you won't want to stutter—but you won't be able to stop."

He told 'Chelle that we wanted her to be a happy girl, and that's why we were spanking her so that she could break her bad habit.

She said, "I understand, Daddy."

After I finished the dishes she and I played in the hallway while Mack bathed. She began stuttering. Through the door, Mack told me to spank her.

Just a few days earlier Mack and I had disagreed and I had not been submissive about something. Mack told me to obey and that night while 'Chelle prayed she thanked Jesus that she wanted to obey and to help Mommie obey Daddy, too! I almost toppled off of my knees. But, back to the hallway.

With the greatest feeling of victory I've ever had, I joyfully said, " 'Chelle, come on, let's obey Daddy." We walked hand in hand to her room. As I got the rod she pertly said, "Mommie, I'll lie across your knees." She offered no resistance when I spanked her. She didn't cry loudly as she usually did, but sobbed afterward on my shoulder for a moment. Then as quickly as a summer shower starts and stops, she smiled and started to play. With my mouth hanging open and tears filling my eyes, I felt that we should talk like we always did after discipline. But I realized there was no need; I had said all I had needed to say when I urged, "Let's obey Daddy." I think my attitude toward Mack triggered her response. She turned to me, and speaking slowly and clearly, said, "See, I'm not stuttering." We all laughed, clapped our hands, and thanked Jesus.

All the next day I swung the rod in love when she stuttered, saying, "We will obey Daddy." I thought to myself, "You're not responsible. He's responsible. He's responsible." 'Chelle responded beautifully and did not stutter the rest of the week. To this day she has never stuttered again.

I still cringe in relating this experience to anyone, and I seldom do. I do not offer it as a remedy for stuttering; I describe it merely as a prescription for responding to one's husband and leaving the results to God.

Through this experience I began to see that God meant even the devastating Mack trucks in my life to deliver only good to me. In that perspective I could truthfully say, "Keep those trucks coming!"

Throughout our six years of marriage and 'Chelle's three years of life, God was chiseling away more and more at the rough edges of my life. Had He cut away the whole imperfection at once, I would have crumbled under the impact.

Probably the most regular conflict in my life those six years occurred at Christmas. I had had a "normal" childhood at Christmas, I thought, with gifts, Christmas trees, blinking lights, Santa Claus and surprises. Mother would usually get us everything on our lists, with a few extras thrown in as a bonus. She thought we would be disappointed if all our wishes weren't granted. It was her way of saying, "I love you and want you to be happy." I adopted that same policy for 'Chelle.

Mack grew up with a different set of values. When he made out his list, he seldom got anything on it. He logically concluded that it was too painful to expect anything.

With two such opposite ideas, you can imagine how peaceful our Christmases were. Sometimes Mack would surprise me with a gift, and other times he exuded as much enthusiasm for the holiday as a turtle at a track meet. One year I bought my own gift, wrapped it, and opened it with delight. I got what I wanted—but not really. I was searching for the real Christmas spirit and didn't know it. Mack was searching too.

After 'Chelle was born, Mack had announced that our child would never be lied to in any regard—starting with Christmas and Santa Claus. His orders were easy to obey the first couple of Christmases. The year that 'Chelle was three, I felt unsure and threatened. After all, her little friends would be talking and pretending and sitting on Santa's knee. What could anyone put in the place of those merry traditions? My whole Christmas season would crumble.

By March I knew that I had to trust God with the problem area or else I'd be crazy by December. I wanted so much to trust Him with all the details of my life, but I was afraid He would take too much away from me. So from March to September I prayed, "O God, if You can straighten out my Christmases You can do anything!

By October I realized that I could no more tell 'Chelle a lie about Santa Claus and make it a part of our family way of life, than I could lie to her about anything else. As I focused on this truth, God provided peace for each day. It was a peace that "passed all understanding" because by November I had not even bought the first gift.

Then December came and again I went quickly to my knees. I almost felt like a reformed alcoholic wanting to reach for the bottle. Each day I asked myself, "Is God big enough to handle this day?" Each day He proved that He could as I patiently kept my eyes on His sufficiency as promised in 2 Corinthians 12:9.

Ways of celebrating Christmas which would be fun and still maintain the truth of the season began to formulate in my mind. We put together a birthday party for Jesus, with 'Chelle and I making Christmas cookies. Her friends gathered with all the party trimmings, and we sang "Happy Birthday" to Jesus.

While 'Chelle and her little friends were playing, Mack and I planned a treasure hunt around the house with notes from here to there for each one. Each ended her search with a small gift found in the dryer, drawer, or some corner. We all had such a good time searching that we laughed till we almost cried.

On Christmas Eve Mack took 'Chelle and me for a wheelbarrow ride around the neighborhood, singing carols. When we got home, Mack and 'Chelle lay down in front of the fireplace, and I brought out a sack full of gifts for 'Chelle. We watched as she opened the items I had carefully chosen from the grocery store. There was a package of flower seeds, a box of muffin mix that she mixed herself for our Christmas breakfast, and her favorite candy. She unforgettably lifted her arms to me and said, "Oh, those were such good gifts, Mommie—let me hug your neck." Tears came to my eyes. Such little things—but they meant a great deal to her.

'Chelle also learned the true spirit of Christmas in another way. I had bought an advent calendar with little doors to open each day before Christmas. Behind each door was a Scripture verse, and it was amazing how many of those verses she learned by heart.

On Christmas morning at one o'clock I woke up. I wasn't sleepy. I wasn't worried—just saturated with peace. So I got up, made a lemon pie, sliced oranges for the ambrosia, listened to a Bible study tape and finished the handwork on a new dress. Two hours' work. During part of that time, I heard some of the most beautiful Christmas music over the radio that I have ever heard. God and I shared a very special few hours; He was reassuring my trembling heart that He would work out the minutest detail of our Christmases.

Our Christmas presents to family and friends brought special joy to all of us. We wrote each person's name and the amount we usually spent on them, then we filled a mission envelope for each one, placed them in a small box tied with red ribbon, and let 'Chelle put "Jesus' birthday gift" in the offering plate. That anonymous red-bowed gift caused no small stir in the congregation. It was like we three had a wonderful secret shared with our heavenly Father. Shopping had been a breeze. Mack had sent me out for a box of cards which announced that our gift to our loved ones this year was helping to spread the Gospel around the world.

The change of seasons, winter to summer, offered new unconquered horizons for me. One good thing I could say about our honeymoon was that we went to the mountains instead of the beach—not only could I not swim, I was deathly afraid of water. Mack loved the water; he had grown up in Florida. I had grown up in eastern Tennessee, surrounded by mountains and seeing few lakes and fewer swimming pools.

Not until after we were married did Mack learn I couldn't swim, and it actually was no big deal to him. He accepted that along with the rest of his surprise package, but he began gently and gradually to condition me to the water. It took me two years to stick my head under water, the next three years to swim in shallow water, and finally I learned to swim all over the pool.

One day Mack and I were at a beach motel swimming pool, and I swam alongside him, back and forth, the length of the pool. I could do well with my body—it was my mind that kept wanting to sink! As I'd get to the eight-foot marker, I'd be tempted to panic. Then I'd ask myself, "You mean your God isn't as big as eight feet." I'd literally laugh up at the clouds. I memorized well and drilled myself on Romans 8:38-39—"For I am persuaded that neither death, nor life . . . nor height, nor depth, nor any other creature, shall be able to separate us from the love of God, which is in Christ Jesus our Lord."

My fear of swimming floated away that day. I realized how fortunate I was as I sat by the pool with a group of friends and Sandy dolefully commented, "I'm afraid of the water and I always will be!" And I said to myself: "That's a cozy place to be—all cuddled up in your fear with no one to drag you out into the cold world!"

Then I realized that my release from fear must have compared in some remote way to the joy of forgiveness Mary Magdalene felt as she stood before Jesus. Since salvation, I had never felt such gratitude to God for my newfound freedom. I was likewise grateful for a husband who cared enough to help draw me out of my fear.

Although I was released from my fear of swimming, it wasn't long until I had to face another challenge. Shortly after our son Michael was born, Mack announced that he had been pondering about an investment for our family entertainment. He had sorted out all the facts—an instinctive trait with him—and decided we needed a sailboat.

Physically I froze. Inside I was screaming, "God, I can't take another Mack truck. I thought I was going to get a rest from trusting You for major things for awhile. Now Mack comes up with this! I've just come through major surgery with my fear of swimming, and now you ask me to go right back to the operating table. Surely this is too much! I can't do it."

Mack stood before me, eagerly waiting for my response.

"Mack Bruner," I said, "the only other worse thing I could possibly imagine is sky diving. And I expect any day now for God to ask me to trust Him for that one."

As usual, God worked slowly and gently in my life. Mack dismissed the subject for awhile, but he was "sailing in his mind." He rented a day sailer and took 'Chelle along. She cried the first time, but with Mack's encouragement she learned to relax and trust him. It became obvious that "Mommie was the one who would be a problem."

It made my stomach ache to think of myself and the children out on that big lake, rolling from side to side. For two hours one evening I poured out my apprehensions to Mack as I had never done before. He was so gentle and tolerant that though he never said, "No, I'll forget it," I was comforted. I even consented to sailing with him and 'Chelle.

Out in the breeze, tilting from side to side in a small boat, I softly cried with each gentle gust. I would have bawled if 'Chelle had not kept saying, "It's OK, Mommie. Don't be afraid. I'm not. "

After a few more times of bawling in the wind and stomping back on shore with vows I'd never go again, I began to see a glimmer of a chance that it might work.

Then all of a sudden Mack's "someday sailboat" became a reality. It was a stable boat, large enough for six adults, with a small cabin, and self-righting leaded ballast. That spelled security to me. Then, after a few times of struggling with Michael in life jackets, pulling ropes and manning the jib sail, lowering the centerboard and counterbalancing, I kept so busy and mad that I almost forgot to be afraid. As long as I didn't look up at that giant sail or see how far we dipped to the side, Mommie was OK.

My real security came as I realized one day that I had done everything I could do—and if we capsized, well, Mack was going to have his hands full. After all, the children and I were entirely his responsibility. That was a very stable horizon for me to focus on. To this day I am secure in sailing with God's provision for me and my children—and sailing isn't bad at all.

Sharing adventures on a sailboat and sharing everyday experiences at home have strengthened our life together. Matter of fact, I'm becoming "liberated" and loving every minute. Just recently, after a busy day, I sat feeding Michael his evening meal and Mack opened the refrigerator. "Sure needs cleaning out," he remarked. Because I've learned not to take his remarks as a personal attack when I've done the best job possible that day ("as unto the Lord"), I responded, "It sure does. It's really a mess. Why don't you clean it out if you have time?"

Mack put his arms around me and said, "Honey, that reaction sure is a change from what it used to be. I'm glad."

Another day, we realized at lunch that almost everything on our plates had been given to us. There was fresh speckled perch from Jack, corn on the cob from Tom, cole slaw—cabbage grown by the man down the street—and fresh homemade bread baked by this "happy wife." You better believe we bowed our heads for thanks! Yes, our country is in a recession-depression. Evidently God is not. I was reminded once again that God takes care of his own.

Yes, I am happy and I am the wife of a happy husband, too. Not long ago I received a compliment from my husband which makes every painful growing experience worth it all. We were on our way home from a friend's house. It was a brand-new house, with grand furnishings to match. Mack had been talking about how talented our hostess was in decorating her home—and fearfully I asked him if he would like our house to be "elegant."

"O, Jan, no," he said. "Never. I couldn't live like that. That's fine for them, but that is just not us. I love the simplicity of our home. I love the way you've made it. In fact," he said, "tonight as I sat there among those guests I watched you. Jan, you radiate a loveliness that no one else had. A peacefulness. An inner joy. I was very proud that you belonged to me. Thank you for being like that."

In his own way my husband had praised me as God says the loving husband will commend the good wife. "Her husband . . . praises her. Many daughters have done virtuously, but thou excellest them all. Favor is deceitful, and beauty is vain but a woman that feareth the Lord, she shall be praised" (Prov. 31:28-30). My Mack is definitely more than a truck.

Reminiscing with Darien

As a young child, I frequently longed for a sister. So when Jan was born, eight years my junior, I considered her God's special gift to me. Even though I dearly loved her, the age difference kept us from having much in common until we were both married.

Once we had common interests to share, I discovered God had not only given me a wonderful sister but a dear friend. Our totally opposite personalities, temperaments, and talents haven't divided us but have contributed to both our maturing. As I really get to know my sister, I can appreciate a perspective opposite from mine, and see how we can wonderfully complement and learn from each other. A husband and wife's differences as well as their strengths and weaknesses should be used likewise to complement each other.

In December 1967 I poured out my heart to God in prayer requesting that He show me how to enjoy life to the fullest and how to share this faith with others. I could hardly contain my excitement soon afterward when Jan brought two vital booklets to me: "The Four Spiritual Laws" and "Have You Made the Wonderful Discovery of the Spirit Filled Life?" These Campus Crusade booklets were just what I needed, though Jan was barely acquainted with them.

In my enthusiasm over the thirst-quenching truths I was learning, I let them bubble out and splash over anyone who come close to me. Later Jan and Mack revealed that my exuberance over these spiritual insights had been like a grain of sand in an oyster's shell to them. I am so thankful that God used my excitement over His Word to develop a spiritual pearl rather than an ugly sore in my sister. Today I realize that spiritual insights should be shared as others feel the need and are ready to receive them.

As Jan and I studied God's Word, she began to discover that true fulfillment is not based on such things as where she went, what kind of house she lived in, or her husband's temperament. Instead, her identity, stability and inner peace are based on her relationship with God and to her husband according to God's design. Properly related to her husband, she is fulfilled and the climate is set to encourage her husband to be the man God intended him to be.

Jan, as well as the majority of women I know, finds it very difficult to accept the fact that a wife's response to her husband's leadership reveals her spiritual condition. God's plan is summarized in 1 Corinthians 11:3. "Christ is the Head of every man; the head of a woman is her husband, and the Head of Christ is God" (AMP). Notice that the woman is not the only one under authority. The man is under Christ's authority, and Christ is under the Father's authority. Christ was willing to assume this position while on earth for our blessing, and wives must assume this position to obtain the protection and blessing God has for us.

Your position under authority never means that you are inferior or that you are to be treated as a slave or a doormat. Instead, it means that God has assigned you and your husband complementary roles in order that you may receive His protection, blessing, and happiness. The husband's role as leader or the head gives the home direction; your role as responder could be compared to a heart that gives life—the pulse of the family. Each role, equal in importance, demands each partner's all—100 percent of our talents and dedication.

Many wives fear that their individuality will be suppressed by being under their husband's authority. Actually, the opposite is true. It's been wonderful to see Jan's unique creativity, talents, and resources develop as she stays under her husband's leadership. She had been freed from fears, impatience and pressures that were a deterrent to individuality. I, too, have seen how God develops my individuality beyond my highest dreams, as I have responded positively to God's leadership through my husband DeWitt. The only way you and I can be free individuals is to be obedient to God's plan for our lives. Otherwise we are in bondage to our sin-nature within.

"But what if Mack is wrong?" Jan had thought when she disagreed with Mack about 'Chelle's stuttering problem. Jan shared her opinion with Mack according to her medical knowledge and her motherly intuition. That was her responsibility, and she did it with love rather than an authoritarian manner. Then she left the final decision to Mack. God honored her obedience and worked it out for the benefit of all concerned. He can do that because His plan is perfect—not His people or their decisions.

Putting into practice the principle of trusting God by obeying your husband can be very painful. Whether your obedience involves a deep hurt, doing something you don't want to, or not doing something you wanted to, may be a process of trying, failing, and trying again in order to break wrong ways of responding and developing new ones. When you see the pain ushering in greater happiness, your purpose is strengthened for the next time.

The better you know Christ and understand His perfect love for you, the easier it is to obey and trust His plan for you as a wife. He wouldn't die to make you a part of God's forever-family and then design a miserable plan for your marriage! His plan is for your happiness by obeying Him and letting Him work out the results under your husband's authority.

Thinking Through with You:

Question: *What role did God assign the husband and wife in the marriage relationship?*
Answer: "Wives, be subject—be submissive and adapt yourselves—to your own husbands as [a service] to the Lord. For the husband is head of the wife as Christ is the Head of the church" (Eph. 5:22-23, AMP).

Q.: *How do you know that God's position for you in the marriage relationship does not lower your worth or importance as a person?*
A.: "There is neither male and female; for you are all one in Christ Jesus" (Gal. 3:28, NASB).

Q.: *Why is a wife to obey her husband even if he is not a Christian?*
A.: "In the same way, you wives, be submissive to your own husbands so that even if any of them are disobedient to the Word, they may be won without a word by the behavior of their wives" (1 Peter 3:1, NASB).

Q.: *How do I know that my advice, insights, perspective and abilities are needed by my husband?*
A.: "The Lord God said, 'It is not good for the man to be alone; I will make him a helper suitable for him'" (Gen. 2:18, NASB).

8

It's Never Too Late

Mildred Brown

I watched in horror that windy April day at the sight of flames lapping through the roof of our store. It seemed like minutes before I could drop my clothes basket and run, screaming the warning: "George, George, the store is on fire!"

Moments before, I had stoked my woodstove to boil water for my last load of wash, and the crumbling chimney was unable to confine the flames. The attic of the frame building was crammed with flammable objects, and in ten minutes everything was destroyed except for the cash drawer and account books that George had the presence of mind to rescue.

As my nostrils burned with the stench of smoke, I numbly recalled that only minutes before I had walked through the store that shelved a special bolt of material which would make a new dress for five-year-old Darien. Now, soot-covered, I stood hand in hand with my husband and silently prayed: *Surely Lord, this doesn't mean we have to return to tenant farming!* We had grown so weary of moving from farm to farm.

George and I were married in the middle '30s during the economic depression. In the South at that time there was very little industry and few jobs except farming. But George loved farming.

I had become a Christian when Darien was three months old, after searching for inner peace with God for years. One night I fell to my knees and prayed, "God, I've tried everything I know to become a Christian. I'm at the end of myself; I'm hopeless and helpless. The rest is up to You." I quit trying to find salvation through my efforts, put it all in His hands, and accepted what Christ had done for me on the cross. I experienced immediate peace, and I walked around for several days with a sense of His presence surrounding me. Though I knew little about the Bible and its principles for Christian living, I trusted Christ as completely as I knew how.

When Darien was three years old, the federal government offered to help Southern tenant farmers with long-term loans at low interest rates. Horses and equipment were main requirements for the loans.

We began eagerly to search for a farm and located one 30 miles away. The agent commented that I seemed reluctant to move that distance and asked, "Would you get homesick?"

I fretted. I'd always felt dependent on my mother after my father died when I was 16 and we moved from Colorado's prairies to Tennessee's rolling hills to be near Mother's parents. We decided not to buy the farm.

My mother had proved to be a shrewd business woman when she was forced to support her three daughters. For years she had successfully managed a country store. I thought she was much wiser than either George or me. During my regular weekly visits, I always told her all about our plans and decisions.

These visits became a source of irritation between George and me. I'd casually say at breakfast, "George, I'd like to go to Mother's and spend the day." And he'd groan, "Why do you want to go there all the time? You went there last week. Don't you have anything to do around here?"

"You know that's the only place I ever go," I'd protest. "Do you expect me to stay home all the time? You go anywhere, anytime you please, and you begrudge me going to Mother's once a week!" By the time we finished arguing, the coffee would be cold, and I'd be even colder. Who could be warm, I thought, toward a selfish, domineering man who would not let his wife visit her mother?

Soon, however, we had an opportunity to manage a store of our own, and I asked my mother's advice. "Do you think George and I could make a success of it?"

"Well, I don't know if you could or not," she said, "but I'll be glad to help. It's a big job, you know."

"Mother thinks we could make a go of it," I told George. "What do you think?"

"Well, if nothing else will do you, I guess we can try," he said, "although I'm not sure it's the best thing to do."

Anything seemed better to me than farming. The crops and weather were always uncertain, and, at best, money was scarce.

After all, I rationalized, George loved to talk with his friends after a hard day's work, and the local store was the central gathering place. He would feel right at home with the daily yarns and woes of farming—the milking, harvesting, and butchering of hogs.

Renting a store spelled security to me. But the fire turned my security and dreams to ashes. Just as dramatically, however, the dream was reconstructed. Within two weeks we were back in business as friends and relatives built a store and living quarters board by board, nail by nail, on a half-acre of land nearby. Their rallying around us was remarkable.

About two years later we had a chance to buy some land adjoining our store. I was very excited about George's opportunity to stop renting a farm and own one.

"George, we have enough for the down payment, and I'm sure we could borrow the rest," I said. "Now is the time to get the land you've always wanted."

He was uneasy. "Do you think we could pay for it?"

"I know we can," I assured him. "Look how well we have been doing in the store, and with what you would make off the land, we could do it easily."

Of course, I had consulted my mother. She agreed with me. We borrowed the money, and the land was ours.

George then voiced his opinion that we should build a house and sell the store.

I thought to myself, "That will never happen. It just can't! I need the store. I like to have money without asking George for it; he probably won't have money to give me, anyway. We couldn't send our children to college or have the things I've always wanted."

To George I said: "You're never satisfied. We are doing great here. I don't believe you know what you want." He looked at me steadily from behind his rimless glasses, "I've never wanted anything but a farm of my own," he said.

We left it at that—my way.

I did most of the buying, stocking, waiting on customers, and pumping gas. I also shuffled our daily groceries from our stock to my pantry with no bookkeeping. In addition, I liberally withdrew money for clothing for Darien and Janice or for household items—with no voucher in return. George, I reasoned, didn't need to know how expensive little girls' dresses were, and though I wasn't extravagant I thought our girls should have the best available. Besides, he would probably fuss.

George had been reared about 10 miles from where we lived. At the age of 16 he was rudely thrust out on his own by the death of both parents. His family of 11 brothers and sisters, most of whom were grown, went their individual ways. It was after this blow that George had become a Christian. He went to live with a nearby farm family and helped with the work. I learned that he fashioned his idea of a perfect couple from the married son living on the farm. She seemed to live to make her husband happy, she was an immaculate housewife, and a good cook. They seemed very devoted to each other.

That was fine for them, but I wanted more out of life than what appeared a humdrum existence. I wanted to do something important that made a contribution to society—and something that made me happy!

Since the beginning of our marriage George had dropped by

the nearest country store after supper and chatted with others for his "recreation." He invited me to accompany him, but I'd much rather read a good book at home. "I really don't care who sold a cow or calf or got their tobacco plowed or set out, or how many pigs Tom Jones' old sow had, or the latest gossip that's going around."

And George had no patience with my reading. "How you can sit around with your nose in a book all the time is more than I can understand. Why do you want to read about all those things that are make-believe?"

"The characters are a lot more interesting and do lots more wonderful things than anyone I know!" I'd retort.

Mother's house had always been so neat, and she kept herself neat, too. She allowed me to cuddle up and read for hours at a time, and so now it seemed much more important to finish the last chapter than do anything else. I could sit right down beside dirty dishes, dirty clothes, unswept floor, and mounds of ironing, and it never bothered me one bit.

Sometimes between novels, I'd sew or crochet, or do an oil painting. I liked to have the house spotless when I was expecting company, but to work for that every day seemed like wasting time.

George didn't agree. He liked well-planned meals on time, not merely something whipped up at the last minute. We had many quarrels over this. When Darien got older, she helped with many meals. I did have to tend the store, but it was more of an excuse than a reason for late, hasty meals.

One night when George came home from milking, I was sitting in the store reading a magazine. He didn't even wait to see if I had supper ready. He just grabbed my magazine and threw it in the stove. I couldn't believe anyone would do anything so terrible. I only lacked a few paragraphs of finishing the story, and now I would never know how it turned out. Besides, I was humiliated in front of several customers.

I went fuming to the kitchen to conjure up supper. I had never liked scenes in front of others. I was completely crushed, and I waited until everyone had left that night before I unbridled my anger at George. A neighbor once said of us, "You think George can fuss. You should hear Mildred lash back when no one's around."

George forgot his anger quickly. Not so with me. Mine came to a more gradual boil and also took much longer to cool. By the time I would get "back to normal" another boiler was heating up, and off we'd go again.

During the long winter months, most of the men in the community would sit and loaf in our store. Many would come early in the morning, buy crackers and cheese or bologna, chew their tobacco, and spit into or at the boxes of ashes in front of the huge pot-bellied stove. On these long days, George was always working in the barn or just doing anything—it seemed to me—to keep himself occupied outside the store.

By evening, weary with work, I'd complain: "George, how come you are the only man in the neighborhood who has any work to do? If we didn't have a store, I bet anything you would be in someone else's store just like the rest of them. Tonight I'm staying in the living room, and I'm not coming into the store at all, not for anything!"

"To hell with the store," he said. "I have work to do and I'm going to do it, tomorrow and the next day and the next!" Then he'd meander into the store to mingle with the customers.

I had become indifferent to George and his needs. He had hurt my feelings so many times that I had built a shell of protection to keep from being hurt more.

I believed Jesus Christ loved me, but He seemed far away in heaven. Then I began to read some books by a well-known preacher. I found out that Jesus was ever-present. I could imagine Him sitting beside my bed at night. I could imagine laying all my problems, cares, and heartaches in His lap and going to sleep with His hand holding mine. I began learning a few Bible verses and specific promises that I quoted when I felt the need for comfort.

Meanwhile I lavished attention on the girls; I wanted them to be happy and have all the things they wanted. I found happiness in their happiness, their friends, and the future. I also tried to protect them from George's "temper tantrums," as I called them. I never told him about our expenses unless I had to, and I bought what I wanted when I wanted it.

As World War II ended and money became more available, our customers went more frequently to town to shop in the supermarkets. We couldn't compete with their prices, and my financial security started to crumble. George began talking about building a house on the farm, and the dread of that lonely life and financial uncertainty brought me close to a nervous breakdown.

Then my mother's health began to decline and she needed help in her store. She convinced George to buy a half-interest in it and move next door to her. We sold our store, and George commuted three miles to his farm each day.

It took us two years to grow weary of this arrangement—it was senseless for George to drive back and forth to work. Besides, I eventually got tired of being told how to do every little thing by my mother. George and I agreed to sell our interest in the store and to move as far away as necessary. "The farther, the better," I said.

So we bought a house near our farm. I was slowly but surely coming untied from Mother's apron strings.

By this time Darien was in college and planned soon to be married. And with Jan growing up fast, I began to panic. Soon Jan would be leaving too. I began a frantic search to bring fulfillment into my life.

I tried everything I could do in our church. I taught a Sunday School class, held Training Union office and served in the Women's Missionary Union. I was there every time the doors opened. I also took part in the PTA, attended Jan's school ball games, and in my "spare time" became a Girl Scout leader and directed day camp.

George began to fuss about all my activities. "You are gone all the time! I'm tired of you running all over the countryside fiddling with a bunch of kids. How do you expect me to farm without any help? You're interested in helping everybody but me," he complained. "It's got to stop!"

"But I like doing something worthwhile," I told him. "I'd go crazy just staying at home all the time. I told you that you wouldn't like living on a farm. We can't make a living here. You aren't satisfied with anything."

That's how it went. We squabbled all the time about money. It cost much more to live than he had thought it would. Darien, going to college, needed as many nice things as her friends had, I thought. That cost too much, too, George said. Soon Darien was married and moved 300 miles away.

At this point in my life, I had a longing to be of definite usefulness in the world. Through our pastor I learned of an opening for houseparents in a children's home. "How beneficial," I thought.

I talked George into applying, and shortly afterward we rented out the farm and moved to the home, just 100 miles from Darien. I was sure God had planned it that way.

George wasn't certain. He didn't like the idea much, but we needed more money, and since neither of us was happy he consented.

I liked it from the beginning. I had my own income and could again buy things for Janice and myself without asking George. I loved the children. The work was hard and many things were not pleasant, but I kept hoping they would improve.

During this time I began to turn more and more to the Lord for comfort and the sense of acceptance that I was not finding in my relationship with George.

George tried to do his work well, but at best the working conditions were bad. After struggling two years, he gave me an ultimatum: "I'm going home, Mildred. If you don't want to go, you can just stay here!"

Darien had confided that George felt I cared nothing for him anymore. She reproved me: "He shows much more affection for you than you show in return. You don't put him first in your life, or prove your love for him."

I shrugged off her comments. I felt Darien didn't understand what I had to put up with. Instead, I prayed that God would make something happen to change George's mind. I thought of my job as "missionary work and very worthwhile."

I expected a miracle—right up until the morning the moving truck arrived. I went along, but not happily. I thought George was leading us out of God's will for our lives, and I saw myself as God's number-one agent to make George suitably remorseful.

Expenses back on the farm piled up. I laughed while recounting each new calamity to my friends. The refrigerator quit running, the well pump had to be replaced, and on and on. "They just don't appreciate God's sense of humor," I thought smugly. I was trusting and praying, "Lord, I know that if things get bad enough George will be glad to go back."

I took a full-time job and George was back to cooking his makeshift meals again. I usually drove home late at night, tearful with unhappiness, and found George already asleep.

Janice, caught in the middle of our turmoil, developed a peptic ulcer. But in the midst of all this trouble, George emphatically assured me that he "never wanted to see the children's home again."

"God," I prayed, "You sure have a problem."

Then George was hospitalized and I knew that *I* had a problem.

We both thought he might die. I saw very clearly at last that he was the most important part of my life. I felt that I could not stand to live without him.

"George, you've just got to get well," I said. "I would be completely lost without you. Life would not be worth living."

"I don't know if I'm going to make it or not," he answered, "but one thing I know, I'm ready to go home if that is the Lord's will."

I stayed day and night until the critical time was past. Then I worked all day on my job and drove the 60 miles to the hospital afterwards to spend the night with him. He couldn't bear for me not to come, and I couldn't stand not to go. Work, money, nothing else seemed important anymore.

All day long I prayed, "Lord, please just spare him to me

this time. I want another chance to show him how much I love him. I know I've never been a good wife to him, but, Lord, please give me one more chance."

The Lord gave me my chance.

George returned home to convalesce. I kept on working. With no hospital insurance, the bills were very high. I tried my best to show my love for him, but I felt as though we were fighting a losing battle financially. Janice had gone off to college for nurses' training, and I thought of all the "nice things" she was needing.

George was so discouraged that he was close to agreeing with me when I suggested that working together in a children's home might be better than the way we were living.

Darien put us in touch with a children's home near her. George consented to an interview, and we were offered a position. But he was in a quandary.

Finally I said, "George, forget the whole thing. There is nothing you want to do but farm, so farm! We'll make it some way, so let's stay here." That was that, as far as I was concerned.

But before long, George was saying, "We really ought to try the job. We couldn't be much worse off than we are now. Let's try it, and if and when I decide to come back, you won't try to change my mind but come willingly."

I agreed, and we journeyed to Georgia—me with a song in my heart and an almost absolute assurance that the Lord wouldn't ask me to return.

George had been raised in an era when parental authority was respected. Although he worked outside during the day, our evenings with the children in the cottage were vexing to him. As acting housemother, I didn't always know how to handle the lack of respect for authority as George thought it should be handled. He looked forward to "better days."

I enjoyed feeling useful now that our girls were grown. Darien had her family, and Jan had married and moved to Florida. Then on one of her visits, Jan told Darien and me about some wonderful seminars they had been attending at their church. We became excited about the "'new" truths they were teaching: how to confess your sins, claiming First John 1:9; the filling of the Spirit; and walking moment by moment under Jesus Christ's control. We realized there was to be an abundant life for Christians as mentioned in John 10:10.

Darien, Jan, and I agreed to have a period of Bible reading and prayer early in the mornings in our separate homes. We exchanged prayer requests. And things began to happen in our lives that showed the Lord was at work. We began to study doctrinal tapes from an experienced Bible teacher, and stability began to shape our lives.

Darien began teaching a neighborhood Bible class for women. I attended several of them and was happy and proud that the Lord was using her. My greatest desire had always been that my girls would be used of the Lord.

One day George came in from working outside and noticed the obvious disobedience and rude language being directed at me by one of the children. This was not unusual. Many of the youngsters behaved this way. George decided this behavior had to stop, and he took over the discipline of this child by giving her a much-deserved spanking.

She was furious. "I'll get even with you," she screamed and ran from the room.

The next day at school she painted a lurid picture of cruelty to a sympathetic teacher, and the teacher pressured the superintendent.

The official was apologetic when he came to see us. "My hands are tied," he said. "In the six years you've worked here, you've been among the best houseparents I've ever had but the lack of understanding by outsiders involving problems with the children forces my decision. I feel it's best for all concerned to let you go."

I answered calmly, "Although all things are not good, I'm sure God means this for good in our lives."

"Yes," he agreed. "Probably this will work out for your good after all."

By this time Darien had begun to study the marriage relationship and was developing a class to teach scriptural principles of marriage. I was very interested in her teaching, but I did not immediately apply the principles to my own life. Listening to her in classes of "Will The Real Woman Please Stand Up?" I marveled at my daughter's being used of God to help young women. "How wonderful for them," I thought. The principles didn't seem all that important in my case—George would just have to be satisfied with me after all these years.

Darien didn't seem to agree. She suggested certain principles that would help me, and I was convicted of some wrong attitudes.

I saw that our last job had been obtained mostly because I wanted it, rather than its being George's choice. I still thought, however, the Lord should give both of us work that we could enjoy and feel useful in doing. For the next year, though, circumstances caused me to rely solely on George for our financial support. Since I wasn't working I had to be quiet and to think. I was convicted of my actual unwillingness to return to the farm if George decided on that, and prayed in the words of Psalm 37:4, "Lord, I'm claiming Your promise to change my heart's desires if I commit my way to You—I'm willing for you to do that if you want us back on the farm."

George had taken a temporary job. The hours were long and the work was hard. For the first time, I sat at home alone, waiting for George to return. Then one day, through no efforts of mine, George was offered a good-paying outdoor job. The salary was more than he and I combined had ever earned! Included were a lovely apartment, paid utilities, and many conveniences. God and George had done it all!

I began practicing certain principles in Darien's course: I learned to genuinely praise my husband, and I tried not to nag to get my own way. George was generous with his money, but, oh, how I hated to *ask* for it! In the deep recesses of my mind, I still believed I needed to help make a living. So once again I tried to make my own money.

I did babysitting in the evenings, and sold cosmetics door-to-door in the daytime. I did not earn much—in fact, a good deal less than George thought I grossed. He began to ask me to buy groceries and other items with my money. He also stopped my writing checks.

When I told Darien about George's growing unpleasantness over money, she said, "Don't you see, Mother? You're doing the same thing all over again. Daddy is supposed to make the living. You are depriving him of this privilege, and now you are having to pay for it. God made the man with the ability to support his family and enjoy it, instead of it being a burden. You need to stop working for money altogether, and just go back to depending on him for everything."

And so I did. One night I said, "George, I've stopped all my outside jobs. I've always hated selling, and other people can take care of their own children. Besides, this is your responsibility, and you are a capable provider. I've been wrong all these years. Will you forgive me?"

Forgive he did. "I never wanted you to work anyway," he said. And with that step, I thought I had arrived. Surely, I was doing *everything* right now!

At first I felt very awkward asking for money, thinking I had to convince George of the merit of the expenditure. Then I learned to relax and simply state my need. He never refused me, though I was ready to accept his decision.

One day at the grocery story I filled my cart only to discover as I stood in line that a twenty dollar bill had disappeared from my purse! "Oh, God. Please, this can't be happening to me," I pleaded. I'd have to write a check and that was forbidden. There seemed to be no other logical solution.

Afterwards I wandered out into the drizzling rain trying to think of some way I could replace the twenty dollars before George knew it was gone. Then I remembered a Bible principle. I'd simply tell the truth.

I braced myself for an explosion at home, but George seemed to sense my dependence on him. "Don't worry," he said, "Forget about the check. Maybe you'd better straighten out your purse."

I felt a warm and comforting fellowship with him that I'd never known before. I began to have a new love and respect for him that I had always wanted.

Our future seemed laid out pretty clearly. George and I would never have many things in common, so I had planned a cozy compromise with as few conflicts as possible. We had been married 39 years, and in two more years George would retire and we would go back to the farm. He could do what he wanted to do there without me, and I would stay home and listen to Bible tapes, visit my friends and relatives, or just be a hermit if that struck my fancy. Surely, that was all the Lord and I could expect. I had long ago given up my dreams of complete fulfillment in marriage.

Then, in one night, my world changed. As quickly as lightning flashes and just as intensely, pain struck my knee. The pain was almost unbearable. For the first time in my life, I thought I was dying. The pain was gone by morning. But the next night it struck in my other knee. Again it was gone by morning. This continued each night, striking first one joint and than another all over my body.

At first, my doctor thought it was a virus. But during his examination, he discovered a thickening in my breasts, and I was scheduled for immediate surgery.

I was sure that cancer had spread all over my body. I would probably die, I thought. I wasn't afraid. In fact, with all my pain, death seemed quite welcome, "My work is done anyway," I thought. "My girls are grown, married, and doing well. I'm not needed anymore. I'll be glad to go home, Lord, where there is no more pain, no more sorrow."

Then I thought of George. What would happen to him if I were gone?

I knew he would be unhappy without me, and I became very sad. I knew that his dream had always been to live on a farm with a wife who enjoyed it and was satisfied with the life he provided. Now what would hapen? I began to think about what would make him happy.

Then the thought came to me: "Maybe he'll go back home

if I die, find a woman who likes the same things he does, marry her, and live the kind of life he's always wanted."

The thought cut me to the heart.

"O Lord," I prayed, "if only I have the chance, I'll be that woman. I'd love to go back home to our farm and live the kind of life George has always wanted." In that moment, as I lay on my hospital bed awaiting the results of the tests, *the desires of my heart were changed.* I longed to go home with George and make him happy.

While I was in the hospital the Lord used my daughters to point out that I still had a lot of unfinished business. Jan, who had always felt that I neglected her father, asked Darien to talk to me.

Darien called me at the hospital. "Mother," she said, "you know Jan and I love you dearly and would never do anything to hurt you. Knowing the pain you are already having and not knowing your prognosis, it's especially difficult to share with you what is on my heart. But Jan and I know that if pain in your soul is needed for God's will to be done in your life, you would want it that way.

"We know that you have made some changes toward Daddy, but we wonder if he is the center of your life as he should be. Jan wonders if you realize the importance of spending time with Daddy, doing the things he enjoys such as gardening, visiting people, or just listening to him.

"Please don't take our opinions as from the Lord," Darien said, "but go to Him in His Word and ask God to reveal if this is true. Again, remember we love you dearly."

I reread my daughter's book, *You Can Be the Wife of Happy Husband.* In Bible quotes I saw God, not my daughters, commanding submission to my husband in all things (Eph. 5:22-24; Col. 3:18; I Peter 3:1-6). Not to some newlywed, but to *me,* who had lived nearly a lifetime doing it all wrong!

I read the pertinent Scriptures and a veil was lifted from my eyes; I got a new look at me and the truth really hurt. I realized I had lived a totally selfish life.

My attitude had been, "George will adjust, he'll get along all right," and then I had lived for my children's happiness, which was just an extension of myself. I was trying to live my life through them. Not only had I deprived George of his rightful place in my life, but I had deprived him of his place as a father by making all the decisions regarding our children. I'd left him out.

I had satisfied myself that I had a good and desirable relationship with the Lord. I thought I was obeying Him in everything. I had hoped in the beginning for a close relationship with George, but had given that up as impossible.

Now as I studied His Word, He drove home to my heart the indisputable fact: I did not have the right relationship with Him if there were any of His commands I ignored or refused to obey.

I had ignored and disobeyed His command to be under George's authority and leadership. The command wasn't dependent on whether George was the kind of husband I thought he should be. It wasn't based on how he acted or reacted. His spiritual condition was not the issue.

I saw that I had the same attitude toward God that I had toward George. I hadn't wanted to be under His authority, either. My personal desires had never been laid aside. I had never trusted Him to supply my needs without my help.

Now I wanted God's best. "Lord," I prayed, "I confess this as sin and accept Your forgiveness. Now, make me the person You want me to be, totally under Your authority by being under George's authority first."

The doctors diagnosed the joint pains as a strain of hepatitis. Although risky, surgery was scheduled for the breast tumor. It was malignant. My breast was removed. Recovery went well, and I convalesced at home. Now I had my dream back: the dream I had when I was first married—that of making my husband happy and being happy myself.

I tried to put some more of the things into practice that I had learned. Instead of talking all the time about things that interested me, I decided to sit quiely and listen to what

George wanted to say. He talked about his childhood—things I had never known. I found him very entertaining and I began learning so many things about him that made me understand him more and appreciate him deeply. I began to find out that he was a much finer, more stable, mature man than I had ever thought. We were becoming acquainted for the first time. I liked him as a person. It was amazing how he began to show respect for my opinions as well.

Recently we moved back to a farm and George and I are both so much happier now, and he is farming as he always wanted to do.

The other day we got a doctor's bill in the mail. Seeing the expression on George's face, I thought, "Oh, this is it! Everything's gone down the drain. There's going to be an old-time explosion."

The lampshade must have rocked on its bulb, and the ivy must have withered in the corner as George blew his top. I felt the old anger and hurt feelings boiling up inside me.

I thought, "Now the truth is coming out! I see how you really feel about me, Mister! You think more of your money than you do of me. If it's going to take all your earnings to save my life and make me well, you'd rather keep your money."

But just in time I remembered the proper way to deal with hurt feelings. "Mildred," I cautioned myself, "confess that sin of anger and bitterness to God. Give your hurt to Him and leave it there. Do not strike out blindly against George. Do not close your heart to him."

So as George continued to rant and rave, I, by the grace of God, kept my mouth shut. What a miracle!

Later as I spoke to the Lord about it, I began to understand George more. Only the day before, he had proudly deposited farm earnings in our savings account. I'm sure it was very satisfying to him, and now he must feel the doctors were conspiring to deplete his savings with that unexpected bill. I remembered his earlier readiness to pay the staggering hospital costs not covered by insurance.

As always, George's temper was quick to flare and quick to cool. A few months earlier I would have carried resentment toward him for several days, but I was learning not to take anger as a personal attack. With my new way of responding to our problems, I felt no resentment toward George.

I don't always feel different from the way I felt in years past, but instead of giving him the cold shoulder that I sometimes feel, I kiss him and by faith act the way I should. Before long God makes my inner feelings match my outer trust. I find that my shell of protection is no longer needed; Jesus Christ is my armor of protection.

It's so difficult to change the habits of a lifetime! Recently I found myself scheming how to divide grocery money to buy our granddaughter a birthday present. I'd buy it, I thought, show it to George, and then ask him to replace the money for groceries.

Then I realized I was trying to get my own way again. I wasn't trusting God to provide as good a present for 'Chelle through my husband as I could purchase. I was also robbing George of the joy of planning and buying our grandchild's gift.

So I talked it over with him and we agreed what she would like. He gave me the money to buy it. He then spent great effort in finding a box, packing the gift, and mailing it. He further suggested that we call Jan long distance on 'Chelle's birthday. What pleasant surprises!

The principle of being under my husband's authority has recently guided me down more new avenues. Since I had not lived under George's authority, I did not trust my daughters to their husbands' authority and care.

It was my pattern, and my duty, I thought, to worry as Mack and Jan traveled the 500 miles from Florida to visit us. I would almost prefer that they not come because of my fear. On one visit Mack said to me, "Mrs. Brown, you surely don't trust me to take care of Jan, or you wouldn't worry so much."

God used Mack's words to pierce deep into my heart, showing me that I was to trust God to care for my girls through their husbands.

The pain of seeing my mistakes is real, but the joy experienced by correcting these attitudes and actions more than compensates me. I'm so glad and grateful that it's never too late to become the wife of a happy husband!

Reminiscing with Darien:

Through my tears, I attempted to explain my emotions to my husband, DeWitt. Mother and I had just returned from the surgeon's office and we both feared that the cancer discovered in one of Mother's breasts had spread throughout her body. Our time together would be short, we felt.

I wasn't frightened of death because I know Mother would be with Jesus in heaven the moment she died. My pain came from knowing that I would no longer enjoy the fellowship of a precious friend, a friend who was always eager to rejoice with me in my joys and empathize with me in my sorrows. She never expressed ridicule or disappointment when my weaknesses or failures were evident. Instead she helped me believe in myself by listening and gently guiding me to see myself and my situation objectively. I could depend on her to understand me when I didn't understand myself. One is truly blessed to have such a friend, and I believe doubly blessed when that friend is also your mother.

As I shared these thoughts with DeWitt, the Lord brought to my mind that He wouldn't take Mother to be with Him unless it was best for both of us. So then and there, I accepted her death. Now that we know her cancer is not terminal, I can truly enjoy our relationship without being dependent on it.

It has been exciting to learn about my role as a wife and be able to share the good news with Mother. We are able to help each other correct mistakes by discussing how God's truths apply in our situation. Growing together in this area has developed a special closeness that we wouldn't have experienced otherwise.

Mother now understands that many unnecessary problems, heartaches, and disappointments developed in her marriage because she did not understand the "job description" of her chosen career. That career was to be Daddy's helpmate, meaning to "leave Father and Mother" and become "one flesh" with her husband, helping him accomplish his goals in life more effectively because he's married to her.

Mother centered her life around *her mother's* advice, direction, and approval rather than her husband's. As a result they didn't buy the farm Daddy dreamed of owning. Instead, they spent years of conflict in a general store, where Mother sought security through money rather than in God through her husband. Daddy's harsh reactions were attempts to gain his rightful place in his wife's life, not to become an over-bearing tyrant.

God doesn't want our individuality to be crushed; He means for it to bloom. It's not our responsibility to change our personalities or to pretend we like things we do not. God wants us to express our ideas and desires. Once a wife has shared her views and feelings, the final decision rests with her husband. If your ideas are overruled, you can relax and follow your husband's guidance, knowing that this doesn't carry either your approval or disapproval.

I've discovered that if I play the role of "go-between" for DeWitt and our boys, their relationships deteriorate rather than improve. I believe my Daddy would have had a closer relationship with his daughters if Mother hadn't tried to work out every situation. Mother, as the great "go-between," was actually a barrier.

Mother now understands that a wife has the freedom to participate in as many outside activities as she desires as long as they do not interfere with her career of marriage. She now has ample time to paint, listen to study tapes, read, and give her time to benevolent services.

The traits Mother wanted to change in my father's life are a mold in God's hand for reshaping her own features. For instance, spending time with Daddy has kept her from becoming the recluse she was edging toward. His desire to have meals on time and the house in order has encouraged the discipline she needed for self-respect. His thriftiness has counteracted her impulsive, excessive spending. His explosive nature has prodded her closer to Christ as her shell of protection.

Mother was reluctant to share her testimony in this book

because she was ashamed of the many mistakes she had made. Then she realized that others might be encouraged by seeing how God has used even her mistakes for all of our good as we have trusted Christ. Anyone who has met my mother need fear no longer that it's too late to make two people one in marriage.

Thinking Through with You:

Question: *What can I learn from God's Word as to how my home should be kept?*
Answer: "All things should be done with regard to decency and propriety and in an orderly fashion" (1 Cor. 14:40, AMP.).

Q.: *How important is financial security to you, and what does God's Word teach about this?*
A.: "He who trusts in his riches will fall, but the righteous will flourish like the green leaf" (Prov. 11:28, NASB).

Q.: *How is God and His truth affected by a Christian wife not in subjection to her husband?*
A.: "Encourage the young women to love their husbands, to love their children, to be sensible, pure, workers at home, kind, being subject to their own husbands, that the Word of God may not be dishonored" (Titus 2:4-5, NASB).

Q.: *Who is the only one who can enable you to unselfishly serve your husband?*
A.: "I can do everything through Christ who strengthens me" (Phil. 4:13, NIV).

Q.: *While the unmarried woman's foremost service is to God, whose leadership must be first—though not final—for the Christian wife?*
A.: "The married woman has her cares [centered] in earthly affairs, how she may please her husband" (1 Cor. 7:34, AMP.).

9

Sex Is
God's Gift

Charlene Dale

"F-I-G-H-T! You've got to F-I-G-H-T! Fight, Panthers, Fight!"
The yells filled the air as I walked into the stadium for the
first high school football game of the season. Girls decked out
in gold mums with blue ribbons led the cheers for the home
team in the bleachers on our side.

In early 1951 my family had moved to Norcross from
Atlanta. At Grady High School I'd been a little fish in a big
pond, but here in Norcross I was the "city" fish in a small
pond. Almost immediately Margaret, a tall, blonde, Swedish
girl, had become my best friend. As we found our seats for
the game, my eyes checked out the football players who filled
the bench below us.

"Average, average" and so on down the bench, I calculated
in my head. And then, "WOW!" The most attractive guy my
16-year-old eyes had ever beheld: tall, with jet black hair.
I turned to Margaret and asked, "Golly, who is that number
12?"

"You would spot him," she replied. "That's Alex Dale, only
the most popular boy in school. Listen, Charlene, he's a junior
and already a four-letter man!"

"Tell me more," I said.

"There's not much more to say. He's a loner, and you'd better forget it."

The game was fantastic. Norcross won 21-0. Alex made two touchdowns, and the crowd went wild.

Afterward everyone went to the gym for a victory dance. As I entered my eyes scanned the crowd, but he was nowhere to be seen.

Records played as I danced with this boy and that. Right in the middle of Eddie Fisher's "Many Times" I saw *him*.

He made his entrance, all decked out in blue jeans and white sweater with a big gold "N" on the front. He walked boldly through the crowd, tapped my partner on the shoulder, and cut in.

"I'm Alex," he said.

"Yes, I know," I answered. "I'm Charlene."

"You're new at Norcross, aren't you?" he asked.

"Yes." And the conversation continued. I felt like the queen of the hop. Alex asked me for every dance, and as we said our "good-byes," I knew I'd really captured the "big man on campus."

I got up early that following Monday. When I saw Alex that day, I wanted to look just right. I had even polished my penny loafers the night before.

I thought, "Well, if I'm going to be Alex's girl, I'd best look the part."

Between first and second periods we met in the hall—and passed in the hall. *Blam;* reality hit me. I wasn't going to be Alex's girl after all. He was nice, friendly, but yet he was distant.

For almost a year, thoughts of Alex took a back seat to cruelty jokes, 3-D movies, and my current steady, Roger.

Then my parents broke the news that we'd be moving back to Atlanta. Roger and I had broken up a few weeks before, and thoughts of Alex had again filled my head. Now we were leaving. I had to make my move.

With my friend Margaret, I plotted and maneuvered. Margaret had been going steady with Jerry, one of Alex's best friends. Margaret and I arranged with Jerry to have Alex ask me for a date.

Poor Alex, he thought the whole evening had been his idea. He called and asked if I'd like to go to a movie with Margaret and Jerry. I faked surprise at hearing from him and answered an excited "Yes."

This was my chance. I dressed ever so carefully. I wore a blue felt skirt, navy cinch belt, baby blue angora sweater and, for good measure, I put on extra crinolines. To top it off, I had my red hair cut into the newest "poodle" style.

When Alex picked me up, he looked adorable: pink shirt, black slacks and a pink-and-white belt . . . Wow! I secretly thought we had to be the best-looking couple around.

We picked up Margaret and Jerry and headed for the Fox Theater. After the movie we stopped for hamburgers and shakes. Later, holding hands at my doorstep, Alex asked if he could call me again!

Though Mother, Daddy, and I moved back to Atlanta where I enrolled in North Fulton High, Alex and I continued to date. For the next year we were inseparable. What a marvelous year! Football games, parties, and the ultimate: Alex's senior prom.

My parents went out of town the first few weeks of the following summer. I convinced Mother that leaving me with my grandmother would give her and daddy the opportunity for a lovely trip alone. In reality, my motives weren't that honorable. I simply didn't want to be away from Alex.

Spectator sports were one of the many interests Alex and I had in common. One warm summer's evening we had gone to see the Atlanta Crackers play. When we left the ballpark, we stopped at my house to watch television as Grandmother didn't have one at her house.

After a few minutes of "The Cisco Kid," we completely forgot the gunfire and thundering horses on the screen. A private house, a year of dating, and our surging emotions were more than either of us could or cared to control.

I was shattered by our intimacy. "How could things have

gone so far?" I thought. I felt that to give myself physically before marriage was unforgiveable. A "nice" girl just didn't do it!

But I believed that in giving myself to Alex, I'd formed an eternal bond between us. I knew without asking that Alex didn't feel this way. And however enjoyable those moments of ecstasy had been, they weren't worth the massive weight of guilt I began to carry.

Between my parents there was no touching or physical expression of affection shown in my presence. At the time when I needed to have serious, open talks with my mother, she completely avoided the subject. In my mind, the reason for this taboo had to be that sex was tainted, not completely honorable even for married people.

Conversations in the gym with some of the older girls became a source of sex information. I graduated from "gym talk" to salacious books that were then kept in an out-of-the-way rack at the corner drugstore. Other bits of knowledge were added from dirty jokes and movies. I felt that sex somehow verged on sin and degradation.

When Alex and I left my house that night, I swore to myself that the intimacy we shared would never happen again. But intimacy once begun is difficult, if not impossible, to end. We learned that we couldn't go from an intimate relationship back to hand-holding. One affectionate situation would lead to another: our lingering kisses led to petting, and the rising passion became so urgent we succumbed completely.

Each time we'd vow it would never happen again. Once, overwhelmed with guilt, I told Alex, "Let's pray; maybe that will keep this from happening again." But we forgot prayer and God the next time our passions were aroused.

Three years after we'd begun dating, I maneuvered us into marriage. Alex was perfectly willing, but I think he was not fully aware how he arrived there. A few nights before our wedding, Alex shared with me his ideals and expectations for a wife. His model was his grandmother, whom he admired deeply. The ideals sounded beautiful that night, but in a short time I found I couldn't or wouldn't live up to them.

We were most compatible during our first year of marriage, enjoying many mutual interests. In retrospect, I see how we ran from one activity to another in a relentless quest for happiness, excitement, and fulfillment.

Our children, two boys, came a year apart. All of a sudden I was hit by fatigue, boredom, and jealousy. Seeds of discontent took root and manifested themselves in resentment of Alex's freedom from home cares.

One by one, the interests we shared began to disappear. We both became very aware of the growing chasm.

Alex felt that if our sex life could be revitalized, the other breaks in our relationship would heal. He introduced new techniques of sexual stimulation that pleased my body but tortured my mind.

I enjoyed the innovations, yet many times waves of guilt would wash over me after Alex fell asleep. Nausea would overcome me as recollection of our love-making raced through my mind. That kind of sex reminded me of the "dirty" books in the drugstore. I was horrified to think what kind of woman I must have been to have enjoyed such pleasures. "Oh, if I could just bathe away the filth!" I agonized.

In time Alex bought us a beautiful new home in the Dunwoody area of Atlanta, and we began to attend a lovely church nearby. At this point in my life God began to move. He made me aware that even with a new home and a good husband there was still something missing. Through the church services I realized that I believed in the existence of a man named Jesus Christ, but I certainly wasn't a Christian. As I heard the Gospel, I pictured myself someday standing before the Lord and saying, "Lord, Lord, have I not done many good deeds in Your name?" Then He would say to me, "Depart from Me; I never knew you!" I was crushed by the recognition that I was spiritually lost.

Not knowing how to deal with this cruel reality, I kept up a Christian facade. I was able to fake out most people with my Scofield Bible and Strong's concordance.

But the planted seed of truth began to grow. Fortunately, my Sunday School teacher was evangelistic-minded and she recognized my Christianity as an act. As we talked one day, I broke down and told her: "Mrs. Sullivan, I don't know what's wrong with me. I just feel completely dead inside."

She answered by explaining simply why Christ came to earth and why He died and rose again. She told me of His deep love and concern for me personally. I learned how I could accept Christ's sacrifice for me. I left her that day with the *real* peace and life of Jesus Christ within me.

I practically lived at the church, after discovering true Christianity. I was starved for spiritual food. During this time I completely ignored Alex and his needs. I lost interest in home, old friends, and family. I only wanted to be with Christians. I recounted to anyone who would listen my story of finding life in Christ. I also did my best to push and preach Alex into conversion.

The drastic changes in my life made Alex quite uncomfortable. He felt left out, separated from the world I had joined. I am sure he must have tried to communicate in many ways, but I wasn't listening. I was running high on Christianity. Alex reacted by making himself scarce. I blamed Alex's lack of Christianity for the continual friction in our relationship.

Our sex life had almost died. I felt now more than ever that Alex's new style in our physical relationship was not only indecent but was evil for a Christian. Through words and action, I conveyed these opinions to Alex.

Of course, I was a lovely Christian wife while witnessing to the unsaved or visiting with other Christians. But at home I was irritable and high-strung, and I continually suffered from tension-headaches.

The ugly discrepancy between my private and my public Christianity finally became clear to me. I decided that if Christianity didn't work at home, it wasn't of much use to me in this life. How could this tension and strain be the "abundant life" Christ had promised?

Then, as if to match my resignation as wife, mother, and

homemaker, Alex quit his job. He spent afternoons drinking coffee and shooting the breeze with some of his friends. In the evenings they'd hop from one northside bar to another. Golf and fishing filled his weekends, drawing him away from home and from me.

I began to spend much time in prayer. "Dear Lord, please help me. I really want Your will. Please lead me to someone, something, which will teach me, show me how to mend the rifts in our home."

In answer to my prayer, the Lord led me to a seminar that taught me many helpful principles. The mood in our home began to brighten, but we still had a long way to go. As I faithfully studied God's Word and put into practice the principles I learned, He began to show me His deliverance.

I learned that a woman is to be submissive "even as Sarah obeyed Abraham." I began to understand that God would work through my husband for my benefit, even though he wasn't yet a Christian.

Richard, a friend of Alex's, owned two airplanes. When Richard had to have both planes in Las Vegas for an antique plane show, he asked Alex to fly one out for him.

Alex told me about the trip: "Charlene, since we would be getting our way paid, I want you to go along with me. There are some terrific shows out there with big-name stars, so be sure you pack some snazzy clothes. We'll make the rounds of the clubs."

"Oh, no, Lord," I thought. But He helped me to keep my big mouth shut, and I prepared to go.

Richard was a heavy drinker, and I had dreadful visions of what was ahead. I was afraid Alex and Richard would take me to vulgar shows and drown the evenings in alcohol. But I recalled the biblical admonition "Cast all your anxiety on Him, because He cares for you" (1 Peter 5:7, NIV). Little by little I turned my worries over to the Lord in prayer.

The Lord did so many little things that first night in Las Vegas to protect me. After arriving, we rented a car and drove toward town. Only a mile from the airport we had a flat tire.

Rain was falling, so by the time Alex and Richard had changed the tire they were muddy from head to foot.

We drove directly to the motel so Alex and Richard could clean up, and after a hot shower Alex lay down on the bed and fell asleep.

I thought, "Oh, thank You, Lord. Now we won't have to go out tonight." No sooner had the prayer left my heart than the phone rang and woke Alex up. It was Richard asking us to come down to the motel lounge.

"Charlene, get your clothes changed," Alex said. "We're going down to the bar!" I prayed silently, "Father, You promised to deliver or protect me, and I'm counting on You."

We walked into a dimly lit bar and stumbled our way past empty tables to where Richard was waiting. There we sat near a phone on which our waitress tearfully begged her boyfriend not to go out with someone else. The piano player seemed to know only one song: "I Can't Live If Livin' Is Without You." The melancholy atmosphere turned Alex off. He stood up and said peevishly, "Let's get out of this place; I can't stand all this depression."

The rain had stopped as we stepped out into the night. The lights of Las Vegas blinked alluringly up and down the street, but hunger pangs overtook all of us, and Richard suggested we dine in the Bacchanal Room at Caesar's Palace. We had a marvelous dinner in a room decorated with a Roman motif. I had never seen such beautiful appointments, nor enjoyed such gracious service.

Dinner and the Lord seemed to dilute Alex's bar-hopping desires. Instead he dropped Richard off at the Frontier Hotel and we began to tour the electrical fantasies. We walked past many dazzling casinos and some of the most luxurious hotels in the world, and just watched other people going about their night lives. The Lord spared me uncomfortable and embarrassing situations and yet let us see the interesting part of the city without upsetting my husband.

Yet the strain in our personal lives remained. I really didn't enjoy Alex's company, nor he mine. We had so few things in common. We still loved each other, but we were so far apart I wondered if there were any way to bridge the gap.

On my knees I asked the Lord to open other doors of instruction. The seminiar I had attended had taught me much, but it didn't satisfy my deeper needs as a woman and a wife. In a few days a friend of mine told me about a seminar called "Will The Real Woman Please Stand Up?" She said she had attended the previous seminar and it dealt directly with God's principles for womanhood. I thought that was exactly what I needed.

As I attended the course, I learned in depth of God's appointed role for a wife. Until then, I had understood "submission" as a response to force. I thought that only if my husband had threatened me was I compelled to obey him.

Darien Cooper taught me from God's Word of a different kind of "submission," of love, of graciousness, of contented willingness. It was an entirely different world.

After each class I went home and began to apply the assignments that Darien gave at the end of each lesson. She explained that we must allow Christ to produce these attitudes and actions in us. As we open ourselves to Him, she said, He will begin making the necessary changes.

I had already tired to do similar things without Christ's help and had failed miserably. But as I became receptive to Christ. He began to change my heart, my attitudes, and my life. The spirit of love began to grow in the garden of our home.

The Lord began to make me aware of many areas of my life in which He had much work to do. In the past, Alex had made cutting remarks about my church attendance. He said, "You spend so much time at that church, maybe you ought to move down there." I never had an answer for that statement.

As I began to apply the principles from God's Word that Darien taught, I realized I indeed had my priorities out of order. The words of Paul passed through my mind: "The married woman has her cares [centered] in earthly affairs, how she please her husband" (1 Cor 7:34, AMP). So I could spend more time with Alex, I quit going to church on Wednesday and Sunday nights. Alex's jealousy of my Christian activities began to fade.

One night I sat down and had a heart-to-heart talk with the man I had married. "Alex, I have just come to understand how wrong my dominance of our home has been," I said. "I know I have copped out in my duties as your wife and the children's mother. You know, honey, it was frightening to realize I wasn't even pleasing the Lord."

Alex sat silently with an "I-can't-believe-this" expression on his face.

"Darling, I apologize for taking control of our marriage, and from this day forward I am backing away. The control of our home, our lives, the whole ball of wax is yours," I said.

Alex, being the dominant type, was astounded by my turnaround, and he seemed in no time to grow in stature with the responsibility I had returned to him.

After much prayer about it, I felt the Lord wanted me to stop my Sunday morning church attendance also. It was obvious that Alex still thought I preferred church and Christians to being with him. I was so afraid to stop going to church altogether that I delayed more than a month after I knew the Lord wanted me to stay home. I feared I would falter in adhering to Christian principles if I weren't reminded regularly by that church service.

Through intense studying and praying, I saw that whatever was in God's will, including pleasing my husband, would not cause me to fall. It was amazing how I was spiritually fed during this period.

I attended a weekly Bible class when it wouldn't interfere with my being with Alex. I read books and listened to teaching tapes. I had the opportunity to hear some unusual speakers on television, such as Corrie ten Boom. I prayed more, and deliberately followed the Lord's Word.

After three months Alex and I were out driving one evening when he asked, "Why in the world did you stop going to church?"

"Well, I learned that it pleased God for me to please

you," I answered. "And I know how opposed you are to my going to church, so I quit. I love you and want your happiness."

He pondered a few minutes and then said words I never expected to hear: "I want you to go back to church and take the boys with you. The church has been good for the boys, and I want them and you to go back."

Miracle!

Alex's attitude has changed greatly, but I still go to church only on Sunday mornings. I know there will be a time when I can resume normal attendance, when it doesn't affect Alex and our relationship. When there is a special program, I ask if he minds if I attend. I try to use better judgment in considering participation in church activities.

Tension lingered on in our bedroom. My fear that Alex's ideas of sex were perverted continued to plague my mind and our relations. One night he said, "You know, I might as well be going to bed with a nun."

The words cut me deeply, but I couldn't cope with my feelings of shame. Alex almost became impotent and I struggled constantly against frigidity.

Eventually I talked with a close friend who was also experiencing sexual problems. I had never been able to discuss my feelings, thoughts, and problems on the subject with anyone, but Sharon was so open that together we learned, read the Scriptures, and discussed what I had heard at Darien's seminar.

Darien said the physical union in marriage was ordained by God for our blessing. "God has designed our desires for the marriage relationship so that when we come together as husband and wife we can share in a physical way what has already happened in our souls," she said.

She talked about the closeness developed in marriage by giving ourselves one to the other. Fulfilling each other's desires and giving each other pleasure is part of the joy of marriage, she said.

I first realized that sex was God's idea as I read Genesis

1:27. "He created him; male and female He created them."
God created man and woman, then "saw everything that He
had made, and behold, it was very good" (Gen. 1:31, AMP).
I had never thought of sex as being fully right and good, and
from God.

All of a sudden it was as if someone had turned on the
light in a dark room. Since there had been no display of affection in my home and the information I had obtained came
from disreputable sources, I felt the whole subject was something that nice people could not revel in.

As the inner light became brighter, I realized that I should
satisfy my husband's sexual appetite as a fountain satisfies
a thirsty person. I learned that there are no sexual perversions
when a wife is satisfying her husband's sexual desires and
needs. (Of course, Charlene was not referring to acts of
sadism.) The writer to the Hebrews said, "Marriage is honorable in all, and the bed undefiled" (Heb. 13:4).

I also learned that I could be a stumbling block if I didn't
satisfy my husband's desires. "Do not refuse and deprive each
other [of your due marital rights] . . . lest Satan tempt you
[to sin] through your lack of restraint of sexual desires" (1 Cor.
7:5, AMP).

Of course, my concepts and feelings didn't change instantly.
But I constantly kept 1 Corinthians 7:4 before me as I needed
to be reminded that "the wife's body does not belong to her
alone but also to her husband" (NIV).

Viewing our relationship according to God's Word made
a complete difference in my response to Alex. Realizing how
beautiful this oneness is, I can fully express my love for Alex. I
praise God that I am liberated now from the world's tawdry
view of sex and living in Christ's freedom of pure love.

Alex is not a Christian yet. But I heard him tell the boys the
other day, "God has made me responsible for you, and therefore I expect you to do as I say." I have learned through mistakes that I am not to do the work of the Holy Spirit. I need
not preach at Alex; I am going to do my best to make Alex
happy, and let God make him holy.

Reminiscing with Darien:

I was eager to meet Charlene because reports I was hearing indicated she was not a "secret-service Christian." Not only did she bring women to hear my lectures, but she encouraged them on the way to class that God's principles really do work. After class they would meet for coffee or lunch and talk about how the truths applied to their individual situations. Charlene was an answer to my prayer that the large class size would not prevent individual needs from being met.

Charlene entered her marriage with "two strikes" against her. She had absorbed distorted views about sex as a young person, and she bore guilt because of premarital relations. Both of these conditions adversely affected her personality and emotions, which are vital elements in sexual compatibility.

Charlene learned that God forbids sex outside of marriage because He wants to protect our happiness. Illicit sex not only damages one's personality, it can destroy the body. The Bible directs: "Flee immorality. Every other sin that a man commits is outside the body, but the immoral man sins agsinst his own body (1 Cor. 6:18, NASB). The deeper, spiritual harm is cited in Proverbs 6:32, "Whoso committeth adultery with a woman lacketh understanding; he that doeth it destroyeth his own soul." Distrust, jealousy, and disintegration of identity may stem from sexual immorality.

Charlene's guilt and frigidity were corrected when she confessed her sin of immorality and began looking at sex from God's perspective.

Charlene's other valuable lesson was that it is not *where* you are that's important but *why* you are there. She was willing to accompany her husband to a night club to please him, but God intervened in such a way that Alex did not blame her. Other women have found that when God didn't prevent them from going to questionable places, He used their uncondemning spirits later to draw their husbands to the Lord.

Charlene understood that she must temporarily stop attending church in order to correct Alex's erroneous idea that she preferred the church and Christians to being with him.

Because Charlene knew that the spiritual food and strength customarily gained at church must be replaced with personal Bible study and other help, she was not "neglecting the assembling" of Christians cautioned by God's Word. She refrained for a time for a godly purpose. And God honored her obedience.

As Charlene concentrates on fulfilling *her* role, God will fulfill His purpose for Alex in His time.

Thinking Through with You:

Question: *What kinds of sex does God condemn?*
Answer: "Don't be under any illusion—neither the impure, the idolator or the adulterer; neither the effeminate, the pervert . . . shall have any share in the kingdom of God. And such men, remember, were some of you! But you have cleansed yourselves from all that; you have been made whole in spirit; you have been justified in the name of the Lord Jesus and in His very Spirit" (1 Cor. 6:9-11, PH).

Q.: *How did Jesus combine compassion and correction toward the woman caught in adultery?*
A.: "Neither do I condemn you; go your way; from now on sin no more" (John 8:11, NASB).

Q.: *How may sins of sexual immorality be forgiven?*
A.: "If we confess our sins, He is faithful and righteous to forgive us our sins and to cleanse us from all unrighteousness" (1 John 1:9, NASB).

Q.: *How does God commend the pleasures of marital union?*
A.: "Let your fountain—of human life—be blessed [with the rewards of fidelity], and rejoice with the wife of your youth. Let her be as the loving hind and pleasant doe [tender, gentle, attractive]; let her bosom satisfy you at all times; and always be transported with delight in her love" (Prov. 5:18-19, AMP).
Do remember: when the principles of God's Word become a part of your life:
You will find fulfillment in your personal life and your marriage;
You will have a closer relationship to God who ordained marriage;
You will discover that you are a real woman—the wife of a happy husband!

OTHER MATERIALS RECOMMENDED
BY THE AUTHORS:

Book:
You Can Be the Wife of a Happy Husband, by Darien Cooper,
Wheaton, Ill.: Victor Books, 1974.

Cassette Tape Recordings:
"Will the Real Woman Please Stand Up"—10 one-hour lessons recorded at an Atlanta seminar by Darien Cooper. The
lessons are taken from the above book with new insights
added.

"Don't Miss Your Own Party"—six 45-minute lessons taught
to a group of Atlanta teen-agers by Darien Cooper. Subject
matter covers drugs, dating, sex, choosing one's lifetime partner, solving parental conflicts, and much more.

"God's Prescription for Child Training"—two 60-minute tapes
by Darien Cooper giving guidelines for training and disciplin-
ing children.

"Women's Challenge Message"—one 90-minute cassette
giving Darien Cooper's testimony on one side and Anne
Carroll's on the other.

"Grace Ministries"—Bible study tapes by the Rev. Howard
Dial. Mr. Dial has taught Hebrew and Greek, the original
languages of the Bible, on the college level.

For information on any of the above or inquiries for speaking
engagements write:

Darien Cooper   Anne Kristin Carroll
c/o His Way Library   or   3090 Rivermont Parkway
P.O. Box 32134   Alpharetta, Georgia 30201
Decatur, Georgia 30032

Inspirational Victor Books for Your Enjoyment

Inspirational Victor Books for Your Enjoyment

U-TURN A practical and relevant study of the Book of Luke, God's Gospel of New Life. By Larry Richards. Textbook **6-2236—$1.75/** Leader's Guide **6-2907—95¢**

THE ACTS—THEN AND NOW Henry Jacobsen discusses how the early Christians were, and we can be, triumphant in spite of circumstances. Textbook **6-2239—$1.95/**Leader's Guide **6-2906—$1.25**

BE JOYFUL In this study of Philippians, Warren W. Wiersbe identifies the things that rob Christians of joy, and supplies overcoming answers to such joy-stealers. Textbook **6-2705—$1.75/** Leader's Guide **6-2918—95¢**

BUILDING A CHRISTIAN HOME Dr. Henry R. Brandt, Christian psychologist, with Homer E. Dowdy, Christian journalist, guides Christians into mature judgments in interfamily relationships. Textbook (cloth) **6-2044—$3.00**/Textbook (paper) **6-2051—$1.95/** Leader's Guide **6-2928—95¢**

GOD, I DON'T UNDERSTAND Kenneth Boa examines "mysteries" of the Bible, explores the reason for them, and explains why we must not try to solve them. Intriguing. Leader's Guide includes overhead projector masters, with instructions for making transparencies. Textbook **6-2722—$2.25**/Leader's Guide **6-2942—$1.95**

THE KINK AND I: A PSYCHIATRIST'S GUIDE TO UNTWISTED LIVING James D. Mallory, Jr., M.D., a dedicated Christian and practicing psychiatrist, with Stanley C. Baldwin, points the way to healing for those common neurotic twists that hurt all of us. Strongly Bible-based. Textbook **6-2237—$1.95**/Leader's Guide **6-2910—95¢**

HOW TO SUCCEED IN BUSINESS WITHOUT BEING A PAGAN How a Christian can run the corporate rat race without trading Christianity for paganism. By Glen Hale Bump. Textbook **6-2712—$1.50**/Leader's Guide **6-2925—95¢**

BECOMING ONE IN THE SPIRIT Larry Richards explains how oneness in Christ can find expression in every relationship of life. Textbook **6-2235—$1.50/**Leader's Guide **6-2905—95¢**

NOW A WORD FROM OUR CREATOR Leslie B. Flynn brings the Ten Commandments to life in terms of what God expects of His people today with contemporary anecdotes and relevant illustrations. Textbook **6-2728—$2.25**/Leader's Guide **6-2945—95¢**

GOOD NEWS FOR BAD TIMES A down-to-earth exposition of 1 Peter, by Richard De Haan. Encourages steadfastness and confidence in bad times because of the good news that God has chosen us in Christ, and will stand by us in life's difficulties. Textbook **6-2719—$1.75**/Leader's Guide **6-2940—95¢**

Add 40¢ postage and handling for the first book, and 10¢ for each additional title. Add $1 for minimum order service charge for orders less than $5.
Prices are subject to change without notice.

VICTOR BOOKS

Inspirational Victor Books for Your Enjoyment